100 Small Fires to Make Your Book Sale
2nd Edition

A How-To Guide and Marketing Plan for Selling Your Book, Kindle Book or eBook, Including Sample Budgets and Time-Lines

By TK Read and Kathleen Vrona

READ THIS BOOK TO MAKE YOUR BOOK SALES BLAZE!

A lot has changed in the publishing and book marketing arena since we published the First Edition of this book over a year ago. The market continues to shift and change. Recent publishing data suggests that some categories are stagnant or in decline (headlines like *E-Book Sales Slip* are all over the media but we could beg to differ on that point as the sales figures capture sales from traditional publishers and likely do not account for the millions of readers that buy self-published e-books) and others, like audio books, are experiencing strong growth.

Some marketing/media channels have faltered (is Google+ dead?) and others have thrived. New business models continue to emerge. Traditional publishers are moving into the indie market cutting prices to compete with self-pubbed books and traditionally published authors are moving back and forth between self-pubbed and traditional. If you can dream it up, it's happening. Cats and dogs are sleeping together.

But what hasn't changed is the fact that competition for readers is growing. There is more and more **content** (books, blogs, articles, video tutorials, Webinars, white papers, research) vying for reader's attention every year.

What does this mean for you the author with a book to sell? Its means you will need to step up your marketing game to get the attention of potential readers. You will need to learn new marketing strategies and apply best practices to maximize your investment and your impact.

So the challenge is clear; what can you do to make your book stand out? Which marketing tactics should you employ to elevate your book to the top of that mushrooming cloud?

100 Small Fires to Make Your Book Sales BLAZE! will answer these questions and more. Inside these pages are strategies to make your blog tours sizzle, your rankings rise and your book sales soar. This book differs from other "How To" marketing tomes in its *action oriented* content. Not only do we give you an overview of the latest marketing trends including **Content Marketing, Antic Advertising and Gamification**, we also provide *100 Small Fires* – concrete and creative ideas you can use to market your book.

And that's not all. In the Appendix, you'll find three marketing plans, covering all sized budgets with timelines for taking specific actions.

The days when authors could depend upon their publishers for promotion are over. These days, regardless of whether you are self-published or have your book with one of the Big Six publishing companies, you carry the load when it comes to marketing and selling your book.

And that load is heavier than it's ever been. In some cases, the publisher will ask you how YOU intend to market your book BEFORE they even pick you up; agents will want you to demonstrate how you will create a sales platform and they may make their decision to offer you a contract based on your answer.

It's a lot to digest and takes a lot of research to find and execute the right solutions. But that's where **100 Small Fires** comes in; after countless hours of research and talking to authors like you, we created this book to help you get quickly to the answers and strategies you need to be successful.

Most of the available book marketing advice on the market is from other writers, not business marketers. This book was written by both a writer **AND** a professional marketer with over 25 years marketing for Fortune 500 companies. We are going to help you think like a marketer by explaining important marketing concepts and helping you apply strategies that marketers use in the most admired and profitable companies. Think of it as your secret weapon for success.

This book condenses the best information we could find, adds new ideas, and examines marketing tools from the classics to the modern day online strategies.

Inside these pages you will find what you need to target your audience, motivate them to buy your books, and transform them into a loyal fan base that will purchase your books for years to come. Read this book to learn how you can effectively focus your marketing efforts so that you can find and build your readership the old fashioned way - one fire cured brick at a time.

Yes, you can do this. Most successful authors started this way and you can too. You can find what works for you by lighting small fires until they blaze a trail to literary success.

100 Small Fires to Make Your Book Sales BLAZE! will show you how.

TK Read and Kathleen Vrona

HOW TO USE THIS BOOK

This book includes several special features to help you find the information most important to you. Each section includes features like:

Budget clues: We present many strategies for book promotion. Some are **FREE**, some are low cost and some will cost Major Bucks. The $ signs indicate the relative cost of the strategy or tactic. Watch for these budgeting clues:

$ As In FREE! Or Low Cost
$$ Moderate Cost
$$$ Major Bucks/Hire the Pros to Do It for You
Fire Starters: We use this term to call out strategies that will really set you apart. Some are based on the latest marketing trends, others are successful strategies used by authors today.

This Worked For: Examples of authors or other companies that used the marketing strategy successfully and how they used it.

Additional Resources: For many sections of the book, we offer additional resources for further study.

TABLE OF CONTENTS

PART ONE:
START KINDLING FLAMES AT LEAST 6-8 MONTHS OUT

Start Your Fire Kindling By Researching Your Target Audience

One of the first steps in creating a marketing campaign to sell a book, or any type of product, is to define your target market or target audience. Who did you have in mind when you wrote your book? Who do you think will be most interested in buying your book? For example, you may target your book to young adults or women between the ages of 30 and 50.

While your book may have broad appeal, it's important to define your best customer or the people most likely to buy your book, and then create a marketing campaign designed to reach those customers. Why is targeting your audience so important? If you have a limited budget, targeting the people most likely to buy your book is the most efficient use of your money. Using the shot gun approach-which means targeting everybody-can be costly and won't yield a good return on your marketing investment. Keep in mind, targeting doesn't mean that you are excluding people, simply that you are focusing your time and resources on the people most likely to buy your book. This is the most affordable and effective way to approach your marketing efforts.

After you define your target, the next step is to learn as much as you can about this group. What Websites do they visit? Where do they go for information? What types of entertainment do they enjoy? How do they buy books? Do they frequent bookstores or shop online? Do they own Kindles or other e-readers? This type of information will help you develop a marketing campaign using the appropriate advertising channels for your audience. An advertising or media channel simply means the medium you use to deliver your marketing messages. Today, marketers use traditional channels like television, radio, and print as well as online channels like social media sites, blogs and YouTube.

For example, traditional mail, newspaper ads and email are still popular messaging channels-versus text or social media -for older age segments including Boomers. In contrast, young adults are easier to reach online or through mobile devices, prefer to communicate via text, and rely on friends and family for product recommendations. So in the case of Gen Y-people born between 1980 and 2000-using a "refer a friend" program may yield good results. If you plan to reach a broad market from young adults to seniors, you will need a cross-channel strategy utilizing many different types of media and channels.

So how do you obtain important information about your target segment like channel preferences? Unless you have a lot of money to pay an agency or market research firm, you will have to be resourceful. It's surprising how much you can learn by searching online.

Fire Starter #1-Seek and find your target segment online.

Find out which Websites are frequented by your target segment. This should give you an idea of where to reach them. For example, if you are writing a romance novel and feel your audience includes moms aged 30+, check out "Top Mommy Blogs", a free directory of popular mom blogs. You will want to frequent these blogs, post, and possibly advertise if allowed. Find below some sites to get you started researching your target audience.

FREE to $

http://www.alexa.com/ - Website statistics-search by category (try searching "boomer").

http://www.pewinternet.org/fact-sheets/social-networking-fact-sheet/ - Pew Research Center's social networking stats.

http://www.pewresearch.org/millennials/teen-internet-use-graphic/ -
a look at teen and young adult Internet use.

Another great way to find the people most likely to buy your book is
to spend some time investigating other authors in your genre who are
targeting the same demographic. Where are these authors marketing
their books? What blogs are they frequenting? You will want to
consider marketing or actively participating on these sites. Better
yet, choose similar sites where your competitors **are not** spending
time or marketing their books.

Now that you have defined your target audience and know where to
find them, it's time to design a marketing campaign that attracts
them to you and your book.

Fire Up Your Online Presence With A Website And Blog

Before you begin to implement a more targeted marketing plan, you
must establish your home base. Your home base is typically your
Website but it could be a blog. It's a place that you "own" which is
important when it comes to the content that you put there versus the
content you publish on others peoples' sites like blogs hosted by
other writers. Your home base is where you put information about
yourself, your bio, your books, your calendar etc. Also, this is where
you typically sell your books or one of the main places you drive
people to make a purchase.

It's also where you post valuable content that PULLs visitors in from
search engines and other sites. How does this work? Let's say your
book is a spy novel. You may write and post content on your
Website about the most famous spies of all time (Mata Hari for
example) or the most famous spy missions of all time. When
someone is searching for this type of content-perhaps they are
researching a specific infamous spy by name-they may find your
Website because you have posted content about this particular spy or
event and you have optimized this content for search. We discuss
search engine optimization (SEO) later in this section. The unique

content that lives on your Website can also be pushed out to your **outposts,** which in turn directs traffic back to your home base.

If your Website is home base, what are your outposts? Outposts are typically social media sites like Facebook, Twitter, Pinterest, your blog and other people's blogs. Outposts are online sites where you have a presence, you post, you engage, you hang out. However, you typically don't own the content. Any content that you post to an outpost that is owned by someone else is at risk with regards to ownership. Think of outposts as places where you meet potential customers and develop relationships. You do this by making connections and by bringing value to a conversation or blog. How can you bring value? You can teach (if you have expertise to share), listen and respectively respond (always) and learn; then re-tweet or share what you learn.

And when the time is right, you direct interested parties back to your home base which is your online store. The most important thing to remember is you don't want to blatantly sell in the outposts. Not only is this bad form, it is not allowed on many blogs and social media sites and will alienate potential buyers. You can, however, direct potential customers to your home base and that's where you sell. Save the selling for your Website unless you are specifically prompted about your book.

Creating a Website

Below you will find some tips on how to create a Website that will attract potential customers and keep them coming back. Your Website is not only the place where you sell books, it's also the place where you develop relationships by offering opportunities for interaction, dialogue, learning and sharing. Remember the three E's: educate, entertain and engage. *Note:* if you want to make reading this book into a drinking game, we recommend taking a drink every time you read the word "engage".

Here is some basic information that every writer's Website should have:

1. **Book information** with instructions on how to purchase; include a picture of the cover

2. **Bio** with your photo

3. **News and events** (blog tours, book signings etc.):
   - Post at least three times the week before every event;
   - For your book birthday, start posting three days before with regular updates on your
      preparations for the event

4. **Links** to all your active digital media sites (outposts)

5. **Links/buttons** that allow visitors to share via email, Facebook and Twitter

6. **Sales driven content** like an author interview and trailer, delivered via video, will attract potential readers

7. **Helpful links** to additional resources; your Website should contain elements geared toward reader engagement (drink) and interaction

8. **BUY NOW** buttons. While your Website should be designed to interact with visitors, you do want your book front and center on your homepage with links to ordering information; include BUY NOW buttons prominently displayed on all your pages

9. **Teasers**; include the most interesting, exciting, funny or suspenseful excerpts from your book

10. Post **photos and videos**; do this on your Website and your outposts where it makes sense; research shows that posting photos and videos increases the likelihood of shares, comments and likes in social media

Videos/Trailers

$ To $$$ Low to Major Bucks

Many established authors swear by videos as an important promotional tool and spend money to create professional one to two minute videos/trailers. These can be used on your Website as well as posted to YouTube and other social media sites. Amazon allows up to eight videos on its Author Pages which is you're profile page on Amazon. For a professionally produced trailer, be prepared to part with some bucks: anywhere from $500 to several thousand dollars.

But you don't have to spend major bucks for a book trailer. Author Valerie Douglas reports using tools like Windows Movie Maker and iMovie to make her own trailers. Check out Valerie's trailers at https://www.facebook.com/video.php?v=1630859736561

To see examples of professionally produced trailers, visit Trailer to the Stars www.trailertothestars.com or the Visual Quill Web site at http://visualquill.com/trailers.html

Here are some **Fire Starting** ideas for your Website:

Fire Starter #2-User Generated Content

UGC - User Generated Content - is one of the latest marketing trends and it can work for you too. Let readers generate content for your Website and they will return to see their creation and direct friends and family to see what they have created. It's win-win!

Post pictures of your fans dressed up as characters in your book. Give prizes for the best dressed. Get your readers engaged by holding a second ending or alternate ending contest where you encourage fans to create new endings and then select the best one and give away prizes.

Fire Starter #3-Virtual Book Club

Develop a Virtual Book Club page and post videos of readers talking about what they liked about your book. Also, ask visitors to video their book club discussions about your book, post the videos, and give away a prize to the best book club discussion.

Fire Starter #4-Video interviews with yourself

Create a mock interview. Write a script for an interview and have a friend or journalism major interview you on video. Post the interview on YouTube: Try going for humor and poke fun at what your book isn't, while at the same time, getting across what it is. Make it random, funny, and/or outrageous. The idea is to get it to go viral (more on *Antic Advertising* and viral marketing in Part III).

Fire Starter #5-Name check your fans

This is a new trend and one that is currently being practiced by some of the biggest companies. You can easily do this as well to keep your fans feeling appreciated and coming back to your Website.

Take Kraft Mac & Cheese for example. The company thanked over 4,000 fans who "liked" a post with a seven minute video tune that name checked every one of them. You should be able to name check every fan with a thank you on your Website or blog. For those of you with a series, thank your most avid fans on a special dedication page in your next book! Discover what the biggest companies have discovered; a "thank you" goes a long way towards creating loyal customers who in turn market you and your book to their network of friends. This is called WOM (word of mouth marketing).

Fire Starter #6-Poll your visitors with surveys

People love to be asked their opinion. This is especially true in easy and quick polls. If your book is about vampires and werewolves, poll your readers as to which one they think is more dangerous to humans. Include a separate section for those who want to explain their vote or cheer for "their team" and then tally up and post the results.

Fire Starter #7-Tell YOUR story; *but only the interesting parts*

Did you overcome great adversity to become a writer or to complete your book? Do you have an interesting story to tell about your writing process? Do you have an unusual muse? Are you the descendant of a famous person or author? If you have a unique story to tell, then YOUR story could be just as important during the promotion as the book itself.

Embrace anything that makes you unique. Here is an interesting example: a jewelry store owner in Wisconsin thought the end of the world was coming and she put this information in a commercial that ended up going viral and garnering national attention for her and her store.
Tell your story on your Website, in your media kit/press release and on your blog.

Fire Starter #8-Gamify your Website

See Section III- *Fire Up Your Book Sales With Gamification* for more information on this latest trend in marketing.

Fire Starter #9-Create contests and giveaways

$-$$ Low to moderate cost

Do you like getting something for free? Sure you do. So does everyone else. Contests and giveaways are a great way to attract prospects to your site and email list. Depending on your budget, you can give away cheap products like branded (with your book name) coffee mugs or tee shirts. To really create a buzz however, you might want to consider a contest offering something more expensive; we gave away a Kindle Fire to promote this book. Priced at around $150, this product fit nicely with our book title. Don't forget to advertise your contests on all your outposts or social media sites including sites like Pinterest.

Fire Starter #10-Add extras

After the book launches, add additional scenes or storylets or information about your characters not included in the book: character back stories; for example, create additional storylets covering their childhood if that period of time is not covered in your book.

Also, add additional research, links, resources etc. that did not make it into the book for your readers' further education and enjoyment. This works really well when you have an interesting setting for your book like Scotland in the middle ages.

Fire Starter #11-Get readers engaged in the creative process

Consumer or customer engagement (drink) is the name of the marketing game. Get people involved early with engaging activities on your Website like the Fire Starters below. This will help you generate awareness and consideration for you and your book.

For example, if you are not married to the name of your book, consider holding a naming contest and use the winner as your book title. This could be risky but also could be worth it from the promotional attention the contest could get. Remember, the winner will help you promote your book to their network of friends and family.

Hold a contest for the best cover art/photo and again, let the winner help you promote your book.
Hold a contest for the best jacket cover copy.

Fire Starter #12-Use content marketing to create lasting relationships

Offer valuable content to keep readers coming back

While you want to sell books on your Website, you also want to use your site to build relationships and capture leads. One way to capture email or other contact information and turn visitors into long term loyal customers (versus make a one-time sale) is to offer a free subscription to a blog, a newsletter, a podcast or video blog. Regardless of the delivery channel, the content must be relevant and valuable to the customer.

This is a good time to talk about *Content Marketing,* a big trend in marketing.

Content marketing basically means publishing content that doesn't look like advertising, but functions like advertising. You're not selling anything directly; instead you give away valuable content or information, while at the same time, positioning yourself and your work in the minds of the reader. If the content is good, it will be shared, and people will link to your site from their sites or blogs.

Let's look at an expert content marketer -Marc Cenedella of **Ladders** (ladders.com). **Marc** publishes a *Monday Newsletter* that enjoys a significant following. In the newsletter, he offers great career advice, including tips on networking, interviewing and searching for a new job. There is often a subtle sales pitch in these newsletters for resume writing or other services offered by the Ladders, but the content is so rich, so valuable for the career minded, you hardly notice the sales pitch. Marc has a friendly conversational tone that's perfect for this purpose. More importantly, he knows his audience and how to pull them into his net with highly relevant, high quality content.

Here is a nugget for you to noodle on: in this day and age where content is king and marketers are searching for valuable content to position their products and companies, who better to leverage this strategy than writers? Creating compelling content that people want to share isn't easy. But writers have a natural advantage. This is your chance to put your skills to good use selling your books.

How can you use content marketing?

Fire Starter #13-Mine your book for big ideas

First, mine your book for your big ideas (non-fiction) or major themes (fiction), and write an article, newsletter or blog post about it. For example, if the setting of your romance novel is Scotland in the 16th century, then research and write some additional content about Scotland during that period. You probably did a lot of research for your book and not all that research ended up in the final product.

Put your research to good use and write an article. Note: later in the book we give you some resources to check out where you can actually make money on your articles.

Fire Starter #14-Tell (another) captivating story

Ironically, storytelling is a hot marketing trend in business today. Business leaders like to talk about what you, the writer, have always known; they like to preach the "power of storytelling" and how stories are easier to remember than facts (duh).

Why are businesses so enamored with storytelling as of late? We all know it's harder than ever to get consumers' attention; they choose the messages they want to hear, they can skip through/over advertisements, are usually multi-tasking, and even enjoying several forms of entertainment at the same time. Intrusive advertising that interrupts our entertainment is an old, outdated and unacceptable model. So marketers are constantly looking for new, fresh and exciting ways to get our attention. They are looking for strategies to sell their products that don't feel like traditional advertising. That's where content marketing and storytelling come in. Marketers use stories to inspire, motivate, and move us to action.

You can do this too. Show potential readers how the magic is made by letting them into your world. Creating stories about your journey as a writer, the making of your book, your book themes and how you came about them, the untold story of your characters etc. etc. is a great way to capture the imaginations of potential readers and create an emotional connection that hopefully will move them to purchase your book.

This Worked For: Storytelling is not really a new concept. Marketers and companies have been telling stories as a way to captivate the masses since the beginning of marketers and companies. Take the story of Harlan Sanders and Kentucky Fried Chicken. According to the KFC Website, "Colonel Harland Sanders carried the secret formula for his Kentucky Fried Chicken in his head and the spice mixture in his care. Today, the recipe is locked away in a safe in Louisville, KY, only a handful of people know that multi-million dollar recipe, and each is obligated to strict confidentiality by contract…" Who doesn't like a story about mysterious secret recipes?

Can you think of any other company who uses the tried and true secret recipe story as a hook? Are you writing a cook book? Why don't you tell the story of a secret family recipe they won't find in your cook book? Better yet, hold a contest with the prize being your family secret recipe.

Here is a more recent example; Chipotle and their advertising agency partners recently won the Film Lions Grand Prix award for an animated film that tells a captivating story about sustainable farming. True story.

Fire Starter #15–Tell someone else's story; form a symbiotic relationship

Let's take it one step further. Companies are looking for content to tell stories about their business and products. Everyone wants compelling content for their business marketing strategies. You are a writer. You tell stories.

Here's an idea: why don't you market yourself to companies who need content and help them tell their stories. Why would you do that? Because it could be a good income stream while you're waiting for your proverbial ship and it will help drive awareness for you and your book too.

Later in the book we will tell you all the places you can share your content including your Website, blog, other people's blogs, E-zines, other Websites dedicated to the topic of your article etc. A final point about sharing your content: you should sell it when you can, but share it for free as much as possible, making sure it always includes a link back to your Website or blog.

The Ultimate Content Marketing- Interactive Tools/Features

$-$$$ Mid to Major Bucks

One of the best forms of online content marketing is the use of interactive features like tools, surveys, calculators etc. Interactive features can help you create exciting engagement (drink) opportunities for your Website visitors. Engaging (drink) visitors will help you develop valuable relationships and awareness for you, your brand and your book.

Interactive features can be in the form of grading tools (see Hub Spot example below), calculators, random word generators, surveys, assessments or tests. They can be the **one thing** that gets visitors to return to your Website again and again or refer their friends. In other words, interactive tools are sometimes the best viral marketing opportunities because they are often shared.

Tools can be used to make predictions, grade performance, assess areas of need, or create a competitive environment by making comparisons. It doesn't matter if it's a health score (think Body Mass Index), longevity calculator (estimates how long you will live based on a series of questions), or a test that determines whether or not you are on team Jacob or team Edward, people love to compare scores.

Regardless of your book's theme, you can come up with a tool or interactive feature that provides useful information or offers entertainment value. Dig deep. Unless you are a programmer, there will be a cost associated with the development of the tool. But it's important that you offer access for free in order to take advantage of word-of-mouse; you want to make it easy for people to share your tool with their social networks by making just one *click!*

A great example of an interactive tool that went viral is the "longevity calculator" mentioned above. Through a series of questions, the calculator estimates how long you will live. Check out one version of this concept at http://www.livingto100.com/. Keep in mind; you don't have to actually create the tool yourself. You can find a tool or partner with someone who offers a relevant tool for your book. For example, if you are writing a book about being a cancer survivor or caring for someone with cancer, find an assessment tool for caregivers and offer on your Website so caregivers can assess their stress level and know when it's time to get help.

This Worked For: Hub Spot created the extremely relevant and valuable Website Grader as a free diagnostic tool to measure the marketing effectiveness of a Website. The tool went viral with their target audience including marketing professionals and Web designers. And guess what? The free tool helps identify potential customers in need of Hub Spot's services, too. After using the Website Grader, companies typically conclude-all by themselves-that they need help improving their sites and turn to Hub Spot for advice. Hub Spot built a tool that was valuable enough to go viral and designed to generate leads at a very low cost. We call that master class! In some marketing circles, we call that type of strategy *Growth Hacking*.

So, how did they get the word out about Website Grader? How did they begin the ripple effect? They promoted the free tool on the Hub Spot blog, posted messages in discussion forums, and submitted the site to social bookmarking Web services like Delicious - which is a great site for finding new Websites and exploring favorites from people who share your interests (Stumble Upon is a similar site with a discovery engine that finds and recommends Web content to users based on their tastes and interests). Finally, Hub Spot commented on other people's blogs, recommending Website Grader as a tool people might like to try and included a link.

A great example of an interactive assessment tool that's all about entertainment value is "The Society of Good Taste" app on Grey Poupon's Facebook page. The app screens visitors to see if they have good enough taste to be admitted to the page. It's an assessment tool that scans your Facebook page and gathers Intel, and then evaluates the data and assigns you a "good taste" score. If you don't pass the assessment, evidently you don't gain access to their page. Note; we haven't tested this to see if anyone is actually rejected, but that's hardly the point!

Fire Starter # 16–Create a tool targeted at writers

What about creating a writer's tool? You can offer a tool that "grades" writing samples or create a Website dedicated to grading writing samples and have writers grading other writers. Or how about a tool that generates character names geared just for writers? What about a tool that sends writers inspirational quotes to address writers block according to a schedule they set at your site? As an added bonus, providing tools that enhance your site visitor's experience also helps you create credibility and support in the writing community.

The Final Step In Lighting A Fire With Your Website…Implement SEO Strategies:

If you want people to find you and your Website, you need to spend some time working on optimizing your site for search. You want to make sure your site is appropriately coded for search, complete with keyword-rich copy, title tags, header text and a unique URL. Many books have been written about search engine optimization (SEO) so we won't cover the concept here in detail. To learn more about SEO techniques, check out Peter Kent's excellent book, *SEO For Dummies.* Keep in mind; you may not be optimizing your site for your book name or even genre. For fiction books, as an example, readers may not be searching for "vampire romance". You may be conducting SEO so people can find the value-added content on your site. See *Content Marketing* above.

Blog Your Way to A Blaze

Six to twelve months before your book launch, start your own blog. Writing a blog is a great way to get out early and begin to develop relationships, trust and credibility with your target audience. In other words, create a loyal fan base before the book launches that you can tap into later when you are ready to promote.

Think of your blog as one of your marketing outposts. It's a place to meet people, have a conversation, build relationships, and serve up valuable content. You can use your blog to offer advice or valuable ideas, pontificate about life, or simply entertain depending on your particular skills and book topic. Keep in mind however, you're blog is not a place to hard sell.

Blogging is very effective for how-to books as it can help you establish yourself as a subject matter expert with your target audience. For example, if you're writing an Internet Marketing book, blog about internet marketing, using material that didn't make it into the book. Don't be tempted to use your blog to talk about how wonderful you are or to talk about your day with excruciating detail including how you took your cat to the vet, unless the recount is hilarious. See section above about content marketing strategy-this strategy applies to blogs as well. Give your followers valuable and unique information and they will visit and revisit your blog. If you start blogging months before your book launches, you will have already built an audience you can market to.

We aren't going to go into detail about the mechanics of setting up a blog. The site below will walk you through how to do this on WordPress which is the blogging program we recommend. WordPress (and other services) include lots of helpful features like scheduling; you can schedule your blog posts so if you're traveling, you can keep up with your blogging.

WordPress.org's free how-to guides:
 http://codex.wordpress.org/New_To_WordPress_-_Where_to_Start

In addition to starting your own blog, you also want to post in other peoples' blogs. To learn more about how to find, participate in and promote in the right blogs to create the biggest fire possible with the least effort, see the next chapter called *Feed The Flames By Building Relationships Early and Often.*

Here are some Fire Starting ideas to leverage blogs for book promotion.

Fire Starter #17-Blog about trending topics

Blogging about the hot topics or viral videos on the Internet will help get your blog noticed in search engines, and in turn, this will help people find you. Twitter's "trending topics" is a good place to start. Trending topics represent the hottest emerging topics being discussed on Twitter. While many topics will be about celebrities, some will be about world news and other meatier topics that should offer food for blogger fodder.

Research the Twitter trending topics or viral Web trends and find one that you can connect to your book theme in a meaningful way. Write a relevant article weaving in the trending topic, but be sure to put your own personal spin on it, and then post to your blog.

Once you post your article to your blog, Tweet about the trending topic, but with your unique angle. Make sure your Tweet includes a link to your blog/content.

Here are some links/sites to help you discover what's hot:

BuzzFeed: Use this viral news aggregator to learn what everyone is talking about.

Reddit- an entertainment, social networking and news site where members can contribute and vote on content. The content is then ranked based on the votes.
Facebook Trending- provides a list of topics and hashtags that have recently spiked in popularity on Facebook.

Fire Starter # 18-Light a fire with video blogs or vlogs

$-$$$

Vlogs are a great way to attract consumers' attention. Remember, video is a hot marketing trend. But only use this strategy if you are comfortable in front of a camera, can find a charismatic partner to help you host the vlogs, or can create a unique avatar or spokesperson to be your mouthpiece. We did this in our video (see it at 100smallfires.com) using clothespin puppets made by the truly wonderful writer, artist and craftsperson Connie Fleming. As with any video project, you can do-it-yourself or pay for professional production.

Fire Starter # 19-Rename your blog to attract interest

Why call it a blog at all? Blogs are becoming as ubiquitous as book reviews. It seems everyone has one. Try re-positioning your blog to attract more attention. In the business world, meetings are often seen as unproductive and therefore, a waste of time. In order to get better attendance, some business leaders have started calling meetings "festivals."

"Come to the new product development kick- off festival". These invites tend to get a much better response. And they may serve cotton candy. Who wouldn't want to come!

Think about your audience and your book content when re-positioning your blog. For the younger, hipper crowd, call it an "Online Coffee Shop." Depending on your blog's focus, a "Web-Based Life-Coaching Site" might fit the bill. Call it a "Virtual Book Club" and invite people to discuss their favorite books. The most important thing is to call it something that resonates with your readers and sounds like a great place to hang out.

Fire Starter # 20-Put your blog content to good use

Many blogs are centered on a theme with content that -over time- becomes so fully developed, they turn into book deals. Some bloggers are now creating blogs with that end-game in mind. So, when creating your blog, think about unique content that could someday be repurposed into a book.

This Worked For: There are many examples of writers turning blogs into books. Seth Godin turned his blog into a franchise of books, and Leah Odze Epstein and Carol Osten Gersberg turned their blog on the interplay between drinking and writing into a book, *Drinking Diaries: Women Serve Their Stories Straight Up.* Probably one of the most famous examples is Julie Powell, who turned her blog into a popular book, and then a movie, *Julie &Julia: 365 Days, 524 Recipes, 1 Tiny Apartment.*

Feed The Flames By Building Relationships Early and Often: Blogs, Facebook, Twitter, Goodreads, Linked In, Amazon, Pinterest, Writer's Classes and Conferences

Now that you have a home base and an outpost or two, it's time to begin building your platform. "Platform" is an important concept in the publishing industry today. Building a platform simply means building a following of loyal fans. If you want to get picked up by a publisher, it helps to have a large number of people who frequent your blog or follow you on Twitter or loads of Facebook friends who hang on your every word. Best of all, it helps to have a thousand people on an email list receiving your newsletter. More on how to build an email list later in the book.

In marketing terms, we would call your followers "leads." So, get started as early as possible generating leads for your book. Even a year out, before the book is edited, you can begin to develop relationships with your target audience. Here are some ways to begin building a platform.

Fire Starter # 21-Target the influencers

Blogging continues to increase with more blogs and bloggers cropping up every minute of every day. While many bloggers are hobbyists, they may also wield tremendous influence. In some cases, blogger communities have more influence than traditional media outlets.

Take the time to find the most active and influential writers and bloggers that YOUR target market follows. Or, active bloggers connected to your genre. These people are important influencers of your potential customers and are worth your time and attention since they will have active communities and a large group of followers. In other words, they have a large platform, which is something you are aspiring to have some day. Creating relationships with the influential people in your market will pay off down the road and can lead to valuable opportunities like affiliate marketing opportunities, speaking engagements and guest blogging events.

Finding these key influencers will take a little leg work but there are services like Klout (klout.com) and Sysomos to help you identify them. Or use services like Twello - the Twitter yellow pages - to search the twittersphere for people in a specific industry or with a specific expertise.

Also try *BookBloggerList.com.* Over 1700+ book bloggers are listed on this free resource (recently shouted out by Publisher's Weekly!) and all you need to do is find the ones who fit your genre and connect with them. According to the site, "We have created this site to help book bloggers find like-minded bloggers and help authors find book bloggers that might be interested in their book".

While blogger outreach should be part of your total marketing campaign, it should not completely replace traditional media outreach. To generate awareness and consideration for your book, you will need to use multiple strategies and channels to reach your potential audience.
The methods you use to approach bloggers should be the same methods you would use to approach traditional journalists, editors and other media players. Understand your target blog's focus, who it is targeted to (its audience) before posting comments, contributing content or sharing information about your book. And always treat bloggers with the same respect you would treat a professional journalist.

Once you follow a blog for a while, you will know if the blog is a good fit for you and whether or not it makes sense to offer your book for the blogger to review. If it's a fit, send them one of your books- free of course-and ask them to "pretty please" review it. This can be a very powerful strategy if the blogger has significant influence and blogs about your book.

Use Facebook, Twitter, Goodreads, and Amazon effectively to market your book

As we mentioned previously, social media sites are marketing outposts and should be used to develop relationships rather than advertise or sell your book directly. Build relationships first, share information, add value to the conversation, make friends, and then drive from your outposts to your home base to sell. Remember, it's called "social" media, not selling media; social implies a two way conversation. Some of the top social sites right now for writers are Twitter, Facebook Fan pages, Pinterest, YouTube and Goodreads.

During the research for this book, we heard a lot of FUD (fear, uncertainty and doubt) about social media. Does it work? How much time and money should I invest? Which social media sites should I spend time on? Which strategies work the best? While this book does not provide a comprehensive review of all relevant social media sites - we could fill another book or two describing how to use all the features on these sites - we do attempt to answer the questions above. Also, look for additional resources for study throughout this section.

Let's start with the first question; does marketing on social media work? We concede that it's
more challenging than ever before to reach current and new fans on popular social sites (see Facebook explanation below). However, we still believe it's worth your time to be present and active on the social sites relevant to your target audience.

First, when people shop for books, they typically start with the bestseller list and then move on to authors they love or have read before. Next, shoppers will likely turn to books that have lots of reviews or that their friends and family recommend.

If you are not yet an established author with a book on the bestseller list, then you must rely on other strategies. One of the best ways new authors can build awareness and consideration for their books is by reaching out and developing a personal connection with potential customers. Would YOU be more likely to buy a book from an author you "met" or got to know on a social media site? Exactly. That's why blogging and social media engagement (drink) are important tactics for new authors.

Social media marketing is not a one-and-done strategy. It takes effort to make social pay off. Setting up a profile or a page is just the beginning. You must be active and consistently, repeatedly engage people with entertaining, interesting and relevant content. And you must share and like and re-tweet and re-pin other people's posts… and then rinse and repeat.

Also, keep in mind that social sites work together and should be integrated. The whole is truly greater than the sum of the parts. They should all link together and support each other, giving you maximum exposure and impressions. For example, your Tweets should automatically post to your Facebook page. Why is this important? I may see your post on Facebook but I may not engage with you until I run across you again on Twitter or YouTube. The more times I "see" you on social media, the more I am likely to engage with you. Therefore, we recommend that you participate on two or more social platforms and keep your profiles consistent across platforms. For example, use the same profile picture on every social media site.

Here are some tips to leverage social media:

Make the most of profile pages

FREE-$

Some sites allow you to create an author's page or profile page which will include some of the same information as your Website. Take advantage of these opportunities and always link your blog and Website to this page. Goodreads Author Page, Amazon's Author's pages, Facebook Fan pages, Google+ profile page, are some examples. Check out more about how to use the profile on Goodreads Author pages here:
http://www.goodreads.com/author/program.

Use your real name

Nicknames or a cutesy alias will confuse readers and make it hard to find you. If appropriate, post a picture of you, not your book. Remember, you want to build a fan base that will keep coming back to you over a long career. All this work should not be about selling one book, unless of course you plan on being a one-book wonder!

Another important point worth repeating; social media sites are your outposts and your outposts should feed each other and be connected. And they should always direct back to the hub if possible, which is your Website or author's page where you DO sell books. In other words, don't hard sell on your outposts, but always include a link back to your home base if allowed so fans can find your book and ordering information when they are ready.

One powerful aspect of social networks is sharing. You have spent time building relationships at your outposts, and this network of people have tremendous potential; the potential to spread the word about your book and share information with their friends which is called word-of-mouth marketing and can be very powerful for authors with small budgets.

This is where content marketing comes into play. You want to make sure to provide valuable content in these social media sites so your network of followers will be inspired to share your content. As you know, many people don't get news from traditional media sites. They get their news or find out what's important or "hot" from their social media networks. Try different mediums for your content such as videos, podcasts, photos and live chats.

Ok, at this point in our journey to book launch day, you have now been out there for months, posting in key strategic blogs for your market, creating a presence on outposts like Facebook, Twitter etc. and building your platform one conversation at a time. And, if you have been playing along with our "engagement" word drinking game, you may be feeling a little loopy.

Let's fast forward for a moment. Imagine your book is ready to promote. How can you subtly update your social sites and make people aware that you have just launched a book? Here are a couple of ideas:

Use Email signatures to your advantage

This is a simple and cheap- as in **FREE-** way to promote your book everywhere you go. Your email signature should have clickable links to your Website or directly to your book for sale. See my example below:

Kathleen Marie Vrona
Author, ghostwriter, speaker
http://100smallfires.com
Want to learn how to market your book? Check out my new book
100 Small Fires

Learn how to use email signatures to promote your book at:
http://www.theworkathomewoman.com/using-your-email-signature-to-promote-your-business/
http://blog.hubspot.com/blog/tabid/6307/bid/31054/10-Clever-Ways-Your-Email-Signature-Can-Support-Your-Marketing.aspx

Tease your followers

Pick a few of the most tantalizing lines from your book and post them to social media as teasers, but only if you can do it so it seems like a natural flow of the conversation.

Finally, if you have your own blog, it's perfectly acceptable to announce your book launch. This audience is already interested in you, what you have to say and will be open to your announcement, as long as it's not a hard sell.

Building Your Personal Brand on Social Media

Not every author finds success through social media outlets but if social media becomes an integral part of your marketing mix, you need to consider that your personal brand becomes a part of the campaign. If you choose to market heavily on the Internet and use blogging and content marketing strategies, the "product" is a combination of the book **and** the author.

This is where things get tricky. On the one hand, the Internet gives writers an opportunity to let readers into their world, and readers may be interested in your personal story (to a degree), your writing process, and your muse or where you get inspiration. They want to know these things as long as they are shared in a compelling and interesting way. For some authors, however, social media has worked against them. This is typically because 1) these authors have blatantly promoted books everywhere they go online, and 2) they whine about the poor life of writers, their kids, feeding their dog and other mundane details of their life.

Don't spoil the magic with the mundane. Readers are not THAT interested in your personal life. And the culture of the Internet has not changed all that much since its inception; people will rail against you if you blatantly abuse blogging or social media etiquette or basically conduct bad online behavior.

Social Media Sites…keep the fires blazing

Facebook

$-$$$ From Your Time to Major Bucks!

If you have been on Facebook for more than a year, you know it's become more challenging to leverage this popular social media site to reach out to current and potential fans. In a nutshell, Facebook has changed its algorithms and pages are getting less exposure in news feeds than they used to. As stated above, we still believe it's worth your time however. Facebook is the most popular social media platform with over 1 billion + users.

Here are **Five Key Steps** to leveraging Facebook effectively:

Step #1- Before you even launch your latest book, get out there and actively participate in communities related to your genre or to the joy of reading and writing. You can virtually introduce yourself to fans of your genre by participating in other organizations and communities on Facebook before you ever launch your author page or book. Make sure to "like" and share content contributed by members of these groups.

Step #2- Create an author Facebook page (sometimes called a Fan page) separate from your personal profile. Use this page for your author persona where you can interact with fans and post about your book launch, events, contests etc. Some authors use Facebook more like a home base than an outpost, keeping fans updated on new projects, what they are reading, events etc. This works well for more established authors. For new authors, be careful using Facebook as a place to sell; if you are just getting to know people, make sure you focus on establishing a connection and offering something of value as opposed to just providing updates on your book launch.

To create a page, follow this link:
https://www.facebook.com/pages/create/?ref_type=bookmark

Choose the *Artist, Band or Public Figure* page category and then the "author" designation.
Most authors use their own name as their Facebook page name. We recommend this or a variation of your name. You will need two images; a cover photo (the larger landscape photo) and a smaller profile picture. Many authors launching a book use their book cover for the cover photo and a picture of themselves for the smaller / profile pic.

Step #3- Promote your Facebook page on all your other social media sites and of course, on your Website/your home base or store front. You should put a "like" box front and center on your Website so your visitors can "like" your FB page right on your Website. Finally, be sure to include your FB author page URL (address) on all your books and in your email signature.

Step #4- Post engaging content on a regular basis; content that is meaningful and relevant and entertaining to your audience. If you are having trouble keeping up with posts, try using apps like Hootsuite that help post content on a pre-defined schedule. In other words, these apps will automatically post content at a pre-set time. You can develop a "drip campaign" (more about this tactic later in the book) that serves up book teasers -intriguing passages or quotes from your characters-every week until launch day.

Here are some tips regards posting engaging content: research suggests that photo posts, videos, shorter posts, emoticons and question posts get better engagement and more "likes". Also, research shows that contests effectively drive likes and engagement (drink). As I'm sure you know it's important to post regularly, especially given the new algorithms. Set up times for taking questions from fans, hold contests for freebies, and comment on your fan's postings. Plug your upcoming speaker engagements or book signings by listing them under the Event function and send invites to all your fans. Post pictures from these occasions. The key is interaction with, not sales to, the people who stop by and visit your page.

It bears repeating; make sure to update your page weekly-at least-with engaging content. You can re-purpose your Website or blog content for your Facebook fan page, or you can create unique content for this social media site.

Step #5- Consider buying "boosts" or ads to broaden your reach and gain greater awareness for you and your books with the right audience. You can pay to "boost" a post which will ensure your post appears on your followers Timeline even if they didn't interact with it. We mentioned the Facebook algorithm above: basically, Facebook is trying to help users get content that is most relevant to them based on their behavior or past interactions. Research suggests that approximately 16% of your posts get seen by all your followers, even when you post regularly. Remember, the chances of your posts showing up on your followers' pages increases the more you post. But if you want to increase the odds, that's where boosts and ads come into play. Because of Facebook's algorithm, the more you post, the more you'll start showing up on the streams of your fan's pages. Likewise, if you only post once or twice a month, you're far less likely to be seen unless people check your page occasionally on their own.

Facebook Ads- Pay to Play

Facebook has a large assortment of ad products to choose from with some of the best targeting options available on social. You can customize the target for your ads, showing ads only to people who have already visited your page or Website. In marketing terms, we call this remarketing and it can be very effective.

Another great targeting option included with all Facebook Ads is the option to show a *Like Page* button to only people who don't already like your page.

Light a fire with Facebook

Fire Starter # 22-Leverage Timelines and Tags

Timeline has some great features to highlight and amplify the most important content on your page.

Take advantage of Facebook Events feature and create a sense of urgency for your book launch. Creating a Facebook Event for your book launch and other noteworthy events allows you to post time-sensitive information which gets more attention than regular posts.

Use this liberally for your noteworthy events, like your book birthday, book signings, important reviews, articles, and so forth. Make sure to include photos wherever possible to make your listings pop.

Post Milestones to tell the journey of your book through words and images. You can create "milestones" for big events like book signings, publication acceptance, a book fair appearance or a good review. Be sure to use images where possible for better engagement and include a link to encourage fans to "click to learn more".

Pin your posts to boost your message; if you want to keep a post front and center on your page, then Pin the post. Pinned posts stay anchored at the top of your page for 7 days. To really maximize this opportunity, include a photo and an "offer" in your post in exchange for a "like" or a name and email address. The offer could be a free copy of your book or copy of an article or white paper. You can add the email address to your contact list for sharing and marketing future projects.

Highlight your posts. This feature allows you to expand a post across your Timeline. A creative use of this feature is to highlight a fan testimonial with a picture of the person included in the post. In marketing, we call this a "customer testimonial" and it's a great strategy to build credibility for you and your personal brand.

When you include photos, don't forget to tag them with you and your companions. While a lot of people tag themselves, they may not tag others as well. When you tag others in your own photographs, it pushes your photo to the top of their photo box (next to the "friends" box) on their profile page. It will also allow that photo to show up in searches of everyone tagged. This means more people see that photograph than if you just tagged yourself.

This worked for: Susan Rosson Spain, the author of *The Twelve Days of Christmas in Georgia*, and *The Deep Cut*, is a photo taking/tagging fiend. She also has loads of "Facebook friends" and tons of people respond to her posts. Does this lead to more book sales? She thinks so.

Fire Starter #23- Collaborate with fans on your next project

Use your Facebook Page to Test Your Next Book Topic

Facebook fan pages are a great way to collaborate with fans on your creative projects. Some authors use their Facebook page (and other social media tools) as a learning laboratory. They post ideas or potential book topics and see what kind of response they get from followers. They may query followers using surveys; imagine if Stephanie Meyer queried her followers before writing the *Twilight* series to determine if fans preferred vampires or werewolves. Facebook is perfect for this; for receiving feedback and gathering insights on future projects. For example, ask you fans for suggestions for a character's name, a location, or a specific conflict they would like to see resolved in your next book. Or, start a chapter and ask your fans to contribute-establish rules around specific number of words, story line etc.

This Worked For: Author Willy Chyr hosted a project he called *The Collabowriters*, an experiment in creating a crowdsourced novel. According to Chyr, "The novel is written one sentence at a time. For each sentence, anyone can enter a submission (up to 140 characters). Users, such as you, then vote on each submission, giving it a score of either +1 or -1. The submission with the highest score becomes the sentence in the novel, or at least until another submission surpasses its score." Australian newspaper *The Sydney Morning Herald* invited its readers to contribute to a crowdsourced novel called *The Necklace*. As the story was revealed online, readers could submit the next chapter of the book.

Fire Starter # 25- Put Fido on Facebook and watch your engagement soar!

No one can resist a dog or cat video, so if you can't beat them, join them. Make a video series starring your darling pet and post on your Facebook page…one irresistible video at a time. Make sure the video includes something of relevance to your book so you may need to get creative on how to weave Fido into your marketing campaign.

This Worked For: Virgin America Facebook page includes an ongoing video series featuring Boo, an adorable puppy. The videos are short and sweet featuring Boo working in the office, on a plane, running through the corridors of the corporate office with a "friend" etc.

Get a jump on your competitors by getting professional help on Facebook

FREE-$$ Moderate Cost

Take it up a notch by using professional templates or design services for your Facebook pages. Check out resources like upwork.com to find a designer for your project: https://www.upwork.com/

Or check out FREE templates to customize your Facebook design at https://www.pageyourself.com/tutorial/

$$$ Major Bucks!

Another option for larger budgets is to outsource your entire Facebook campaign. Check out this site for information on some of the leading social media marketing services. These experts will help you build a fan page and strategies to get the most from Facebook: http://social-media-marketing-services-review.toptenreviews.com/

For additional information on using Facebook including great ideas and examples of how other authors leverage Facebook: http://www.writeontrack.ie/facebook-2/how-writers-can-sell-more-books-on-facebook/

GOOGLE+
$ Little to No Cost

Google+ is owned by Google Inc. and is a social networking site like Facebook. At least that's the simple explanation of what Google+ is or was all about. We would give you the more complete and nuanced description of all Google+ has to offer except that it may be changing soon. Google recently announced that they plan to re-organize Google+. In other words, Google+ is in a state of transition and based on company statements, the consensus on the street is that Google+ is getting out of the social networking business and focusing instead on key products or platforms like Hangouts and Photos.

To learn more about the future of Google+, you can find the "official Google blog" at https://googleblog.blogspot.com/2015/07/everything-in-its-right-place.html

Given these recent developments, if you are not on Google+ yet, you might want to wait until Googles intentions are fully known and there is more clarity about the future of Google+. In the meantime however, we do recommend you consider Hangouts as a tool to video-conference with your fans. Again, based on recent company statements, it looks like this is a product that Google will continue to support. See below for more on how to start a fire with Hangouts.

If you are already on Google+ and trying to decide if you should invest more/less time building a platform there, consider these important points.

While data on the use of Google+ are not publicly available from Google itself, a recent study conducted by Stone Temple Consulting in April 2015 suggests that Google+ doesn't have nearly the number of active users that Facebook or other social tools (Twitter) have. According to this study, "active profiles on Google+ amount to 111 million users and only 6.7 million users have 50 or more posts ever". Compare this to the number of active users on Facebook which is purported to be in the range of 800+ million to a billion. Remember, comparing "users" or members isn't really helpful. When comparing social media platforms, the numbers you want to focus on are for "active" users.

Google has a track record of abruptly canceling social media products that haven't met market expectations. We commented on this in the last edition of this book and directed you to the somewhat humorous visual depiction of deleted Google apps and programs at the Google Graveyard on Pinterest: http://pinterest.com/googlegraveyard/google-graveyard/.

Finally, it's been reported (remember not much data exists on users from Google itself) that the majority of people- up to 70%- on Google+ today are primarily tech savvy males aged 24 to 36. These tend to be professionals who work in the engineering and software industries and are more interested in discussing like interests versus sharing family photos. So, add this fact to all the above and you have to question making any type of investment (time or money) marketing on this site, unless of course your audience is tech savvy males aged 24 to 36!

We do however recommend that you keep a close eye on Google+ as this platform evolves. If the company does continue to grow this site as a social networking platform, it may be worth your time. Here's why: Google+ may become a better platform for finding like-minded writers (to share information, marketing tips etc.) and readers who are interested in your genre given the current culture is more focused on connecting people with mutual interests. In comparison, Facebook was grown on the premise of connecting people to their past or to current friends and family.

Now back to Hangouts; as we said above, Google has indicated that Hangouts will be a focus for the company moving forward. As an author marketing a book, there is a lot to love about Hangouts.

Hangouts is a video chat service that allows up to 10 users to chat LIVE at the same time for FREE. In other words, you can interact in real time with your target audience. Earlier in this book we talked about the power of video. Video conferencing allows you to make a personal connection with your target audience and it's more engaging than say a blog. People are more likely to trust you as a writer and take a chance on your book if they can see you and engage with you virtually in person. It's a proven fact; people are more inclined to buy a book, a piece of art, or other creations when they have a chance to meet the artist /writer.

We used Hangouts to launch the first edition of this book by hosting a casual "hangout" with other writers who expressed interest in learning more about our book and sharing marketing tips with each other. We found it to be an easy and inexpensive (FREE) promotional tool. This is a great use of Hangouts; host casual meetings with your writer friends to connect and support each other and share marketing "best practices" before your book launch. You can test Hangouts in a safe environment with your writer friends and get comfortable in front of the camera.

Fire Starter # 25- Leverage Google Hangouts for your Book Launch

FREE to $

In the months leading up to your book launch, you can build excitement by hosting a Hangout each time you reach a key milestone.

Plan a virtual book tour and save money by hosting virtual book readings in a variety of cities. Share excerpts of your book and intermingle stories of your writing process, how you created lead characters (are they based on people you know?) and share the story of your muse.

If you are having a hard time getting the word out about your Hangouts to new fans, contact your current fans, let them know that you plan to share plot ideas from your next project and you want their feedback and encourage them to bring a friend. After discussing your next project, let everyone know about your new book/book launch.

Another opportunity to leverage Hangouts is to create a "meet and greet" with key influencers. It's an opportunity for influencers to meet the author and ask questions. For example, members of the local press, influential bloggers, and owners of book stores, other writers who may be able to help you market your book etc. You may want to host a Hangout just for these folks and call it "Meet the Author".

Fire Starter # 26- Use *Hangouts on Air* to Create Excitement with Live Broadcasts

With Hangouts on Air, you can broadcast live discussions or "presentations" to the public through your Google+ page and YouTube channel. If the "live" part of this equation makes you nervous, you can also record and edit presentations sharing them later through your Website, blog etc. So, in essence, the tool allows you to create and share videos that can educate, entertain and draw people into your moments of writing magic. Best of all, you can do this inexpensively and with little to no technical skills.

What's the major difference between a Hangout and a Hangout on Air? A Hangout on Air is broadcast publicly through your YouTube channel which limits direct interaction while a regular Hangout is usually used for smaller groups for more intimate and interactive discussions.

Also, you are not able to record a regular Hangout and it will not be broadcast through your YouTube channel.

We covered the power of videos earlier and we will talk more about YouTube as a marketing tool later in this book. Following are some repeat and new ideas.

You can create and post videos on the writing process and your journey from book idea to book launch. These video diaries can draw people into your world and get them hooked and excited for your book launch.

If you create a "panel" and host a discussion, you don't have to be the star of your videos. Get your fans involved and invite them to a virtual book club meeting where you discuss characters, plot points or the ending of your book. Host an alternate ending discussion and explore other possible endings to your book.

If you are marketing a cookbook, broadcast a live "event" featuring you (or someone more skilled at live video presentations) cooking a recipe from your book.

With both Hangouts and Hangouts on Air you get the following features, which can be applied creatively as marketing tools: videoconferencing, screen sharing (allows you to share your computer screen or look at someone else's screen), chat and document sharing. Chat allows people viewing your live Hangout on Air to send messages or questions. Document sharing could be used to co-create an outline of your next project with your fans during a Hangout which gives them a behind-the-curtains look at the writing process.

Twitter

Free to $

Twitter is a superb "instant messaging" platform and tweeting regularly is a great way to hone your skill at crafting short (140 characters or less) pithy messages that are intriguing enough to drive clicks, shares and retweets. Authors can use Twitter to connect with fans, readers, and other writers etc. just like you use other social media platforms. Some authors, who have been in the Twittersphere for some time, suggest that Twitter works better as a micro blog than as a portal to drive traffic to a Website.

The best way to understand how Twitter is working for you is to leverage Twitter Analytics. Twitter offers lots of helpful data about your tweets and "how they resonate with your audience". You can click on any tweet and learn how many times people clicked it or shared it. You can also discover the number of re-tweets, replies and follows. To access your data, log on to analytics.twitter.com with your Twitter username and password to turn on analytics for your account.

If you are not getting the engagement (drink…how are we feeling?) you want with your Twitter posts, here are some tips to get more impressions and overall better engagement (drink…should we stop?) with your tweets. Note: "engagement" (we cannot continue to promote drinking) simply means the number of times a user has interacted with your tweet including clicks. It does NOT mean "an opportunity to take a drink". Just wanted to clear that up.

First, Twitter itself states that tweets with images drive more engagement and generate more response. Enough said.

Also, puns, humor, and quotes get better engagement on Twitter; people want to be entertained or inspired on Twitter. They don't want to hear about your day or what you had for dinner. Find some that are relevant to your book topic and tweet them.

Keep your tweets short and sweet; research suggests that tweets in the 110 character range get better engagement than ones that max out at 140 characters. One reason; keeping your tweets slim and trim allows room for others to retweet your tweet and add comments.

Don't forget to tweet about trending topics; again, look for hot topics that have some relevance to your book theme. Twitter is all about real time so make sure you are following and tweeting about what's trending on Twitter NOW.

Make it super easy for people to engage with your tweets by including links and hash tags. Leverage trending Twitter hash tags in your posts to boost your messages. This will help you reach people outside your current circle of followers. Everyone discussing that topic or following that hash tag will see your post. The Twitter Website offers information on the top trending hash tags. However, don't go crazy. Research suggests that using more than two hash tags per tweet actually causes a reduction in engagement.

Finally, encourage sharing. Don't be coy about it. Combine a compelling tip with a great photo and add a message like "Share this with anyone you think can use this tip." Include a call to action; ask for retweets by simply …well…asking; **"please retweet".**

Some authors separate their personal profile from their author persona on Twitter. Try opening a separate account for your book. Example: @100SmallFires. This way, you can keep your activity focused on developing relationships that will help you promote your books and build a platform with your intended audience. Start following people and organizations that may comprise your readership. Keep your tweets as focused as possible by making sure they are connected and relevant to your book topic, while at the same time entertaining or educational and share worthy. Don't forget to follow other writers in your genre to see what's working for them.

The culture of Twitter is similar to other social media sites in that Twitter relationships often develop when readers "pay it forward" with retweets, mentioning others while using hash tags, and simply responding to others. Read other's tweets and retweet those you think have merit.

A hash tag is a way to organize conversations. For example, the hash tag #fridayfollows is used by people on Fridays to thank those who follow them on Twitter. If you want to see who others are following, you can search the hash tag, and you'll see a list of people who are using the tag and posting near the time of your search.

Another important tip to generate more followers and impressions is to answer all Tweets mentioning you or addressed to you, and follow all people who follow you, at least all the people you want in your network, or you feel comfortable following.

Fire Starter # 27-Introduce your characters to the Twittersphere

If you are a fiction writer, open an account for the name of your main character or your villain, or both. Tweet in the voice of your characters and have dialogue between them and yourself as the writer.

This Worked For: Laurie R. King has an account in the name of Mary Russell, the main character for her book *The Beekeeper's Apprentice*. To see how this works for her, click here: https://twitter.com/mary_russell.

Pinterest

Free to $

Pinterest is a cork board social media site where participants share their interests by pinning pictures or content on their pages. With visually stimulating images, you can communicate ideas about your book or characters that words alone cannot convey. At present, Pinterest ranks behind Facebook and Twitter as the third largest social media site, so it's worth investigating. The best way to understand the creative potential of Pinterest is to go there. As they say, a picture is worth a thousand words: www.pinterest.com

Recently, Pinterest installed categories to organize pages. Books are in a category that also includes film and music. Check it out here: https://www.pinterest.com/categories/film_music_books/

Visit the Pinterest "Goodies" page for **FREE** marketing tools like Pinterest widgets that help Pinners follow and share your work.

Here are some ways to fire up Pinterest for book marketing sizzle:

Fire Starter # 28-Use vibrant images to bring your book to life

Have you ever read a book and thought, "I wish there were pictures??" This is a great place to bring your book to life with images. Make a board for each of your books and pin pictures of images associated with their themes, characters, plots and settings.

Make a pin board collage for each character. Pin images that reflect that character's interests, lifestyle, hopes and dreams. This is a place to show off your characters' personality. Think of it as an extension of the book. Let your readers pin images they feel reflect the character as well. This could provide some interesting insights for future books if you are writing a series. You may be surprised to learn how your readers view your characters.

Fire Starter # 29-Use Pinterest features for social media synchronicity.

Take time to fill out your profile thoroughly, including pictures, links to your Website and other social media sites. Forget the "About" section. This is a great way to connect all your social media sites and leverage the growth of Pinterest.

In addition, Pinterest lets authors make badges with links to their Website or other sales site that people can pin up on their pages so others can see them. Go to http://pinterest.com/about/goodies/ and make a badge for each of your books and/or main characters. If you have a Word Press blog, you can use a widget for this. Find it here: http://wordpress.org/extend/plugins/pinterest-rss-widget/.

Add visually interesting pictures to your blog posts and Website, then pin them on your board. This will direct readers from your blog/Website to your Pinterest board and your Pinterest board viewers to your blog/site.

Fire Starter # 30-"Like" others and they will "Like" you back.

Your Pinterest content can go viral just like content on other social media sites. Interact with others by "liking" their pins, re-pinning their pins on your board and tagging them on your board where appropriate. Hopefully, others will reciprocate. Pinterest displays the most "liked" and re-pinned images on a "Popular" page. This is a great opportunity for exposure and to build awareness for your book.

Fire Starter # 31-Repurpose your video content for maximum exposure

Pin your book trailer, an author interview, or an interview with one of your characters to the Pinterest Video category.

A word of caution: Be wary of copyright when pinning or re-pinning pictures. Copyright violations abound on Pinterest, mostly because people don't realize they may be pinning someone's creative work without permission. Just because someone pinned a picture first, doesn't mean they had a license to do so, and if you re-pin it, you'll be violating copyright too! Avoid this by using your own photographs, and by re-pinning works you know to be from the original creator's boards. Also note, by placing your own photos on Pinterest, you are allowing others to re-pin them.

You Tube

Free to $

There are many reasons to consider YouTube for marketing even if you are less than enthusiastic about being the star of your videos. With its free-to-use business model and broad reach, we think YouTube has enormous appeal as a marketing platform for authors.

Furthermore, videos are highly ranked in Google's searches; don't forget, Google owns YouTube. We have already talked extensively in this book on the power of video to engage people, tell stories, create an emotional connection and build trust. If people "know" and trust you, they are more likely to buy your book.

Let's start with some key stats. According to the YouTube Website, YouTube has over a billion users –almost a third of all people on the Internet- and every day, people watch hundreds of millions of hours of YouTube videos and generate billions of views? Who is the audience watching all those videos? The platform enjoys a broad demographic reach, including both male and females and young and old alike. Males watch LOTS of gaming videos, but if you pull out that category, it's a pretty even split. The sweet spot is 18- 24 as this segment logs lots of hours on YT. YouTube overall reaches more 18-49 year olds than any cable network in the U.S.

To get started with YouTube, create an YT channel and include all your social media links. A "channel" on YouTube is basically the same as a Facebook page or a profile on Pinterest. Next, create a 1-3 minute book trailer (see section on book trailers earlier in this book), and upload to your channel. Now that you have a presence and a video, you can begin to engage with users of the site. YT is like any other social media site in that you want to engage with other users and other people's content. Be sure to "favorite" relevant videos and make YT "friends."

Now it's time to expand into additional videos. If you have written a "how to" book or a cookbook, for example, use the content for the book to create an educational video or cooking demonstration. Make sure and categorize your videos (YT offers about 15 categories) and add relevant "tags" so people can find them.

Finally, promote your videos by talking about them on all your social media sites: blogging about it, tweeting about it, or adding it to your FB page.

Here are some additional ideas for creating compelling video content, some of which we covered earlier in this book. Ask one of your super fans to create a customer testimonial. Ask them to create a video talking about your book and why they liked it. Create a mock interview; write a script and have someone "interview" you on camera. Alternatively, ask your fans to submit questions and video yourself giving the answers. Flip that idea and interview your fans, record their responses. Record yourself reading the most exciting chapters of your book. Every time you speak at any type of event, make sure there is a video camera. This is great content for all your social media platforms. Create short videos on your writing process. For some inspiration, sign up for James Patterson's Master Class online and check out James's videos where he talks about his writing process. Don't forget that you can post your Hangouts or Hangouts on Air to YT.

Make sure to include a call to action in your videos. Ask people to like or share your video or ask them to visit your Website to learn more about your book.

How do you get the word out about your videos? Begin by telling your current fans, friends and others in your personal network. Furthermore, post your videos on your other social media sites. Share links in your email signature.

Fire Starter # 32-Let your fans ACT out!

Everyone loves a contest, and everyone likes to see themselves on the big screen. So, run a contest and offer a prize for the best acted-out chapter/scene from your book. Encourage your current fans (if you don't have any, get the party started with your family and friends) to create and submit videos of them dressed as your characters and acting-out the most exciting scenes from your book. Load the winning entry to YouTube or better yet, load them all and get viewers to vote.

Another twist on this strategy is to select fans to enter the contest. Treat them as insiders and make them feel special by "selecting" your super fans to participate in an "exclusive" contest. This is a nice way to reward your super fans (make sure the prize is worthy of the cause) while at the same time developing fun content that can then be shared and hopefully viewed by new readers.

Other social media opportunities

HubPages and Listverse

Free to Make Some Money!

HubPages and Listverse are two examples of sites that will pay writers for content that becomes popular with their audience. While the opportunity to make money is certainly attractive, we include these sites in this book because they represent an opportunity for you to build awareness for you as an author and for your book. As you can see, this is a great way for authors to get exposure to readers or potential book buyers. This strategy is especially compelling if you are promoting a non-fiction book. If you publish articles that are relevant to your current book, you can establish yourself as an expert who in turn will build trust with readers. You can turn HubPages readers into book buying fans.

HubPages is a platform for writers to publish articles about basically any topic and potentially earn money, recognition and readership. According to HubPages homepage, "Hubbers find and build an audience, easily create articles, and earn all sorts of rewards, from accolades to ad revenue. *Over 27 million people explore HubPages every month.*"Authors upload original content - that's not published anywhere else-, and the content becomes search enabled.

How do you make money on HubPages? If your content is popular, you can earn money from ads placed within the content; HubPages shares 60% of the ad revenue with the writer.

Listverse is just what it sounds like; it's all about the list and everyone loves a list; *Top Ten Diets, Five Things Preventing You*

From Becoming a Millionaire, etc. We call this "link bait" or content designed to attract attention and links. At Listverse, you can submit lists with compelling or unknown and fascinating facts and make money if your list makes the cut; they pay $100 for every list they publish. According to Listverse, they are the original Top Ten sites "offering Top-10 Lists of everything under the sun. We give you the most fascinating gems of human knowledge. Four fact-packed top ten lists daily." They claim to serve over 30 million pages a month to more than 8 million readers and publish lists that specialize in the bizarre or lesser-known trivia. In other words, this is just the kind of thing that could help get an unknown author some recognition. Every book has at least one good associated list. Dig deep. This could be the **one thing** that propels you into the hearts and minds of potential book buyers.

Groupon, Living Social, My Daily Thread

Fire Starter # 33-Use collective buying sites for maximum sales exposure

Consider selling your book on collective buying or group buying sites like *Groupon, Living Social, My Daily Thread* and *Deal On.* These sites continue to grow in popularity and offer you another channel to build awareness and sell your book through incentives. You can customize your offer by market. Think about offering your book packaged with other items for book clubs or parties.

Warning: Price your packages to include reasonable profit; factor in packaging and shipping and limit it to a number that you can manage or this Fire Starter can become a Fire Burner.

Writers' Groups, Classes, and Conferences

$$ to $$$ Mid-to-Major Bucks

Social media and online sites are not the only places you should be frequenting to build relationships and your platform before your book launches. Join a writers' group or take a writing class. Consider other writers your support group; help them and they will help you back.

100 days out from your book's birthday, take a class where you polish up the first crucial pages of your book with help from a teacher and other writers. Not only will this help improve the quality of your book, you may bond with some of the other writers. If you hit it off with some of them, when you're ready, you can ask them to read the rest of your book and even write a review.

Classes such as these are offered by colleges and online providers like www.mediabistro.com and Writer's Digest, as well as many other organizations. In the 100 days leading up to your book launch, attend as many book-signings in your area as you can. Support other local authors and they will support you back. Get involved in writing organizations by volunteering at conferences and writing for newsletters. Attend at least one writing conference and soft sell by passing out cards. Offer to be the "forum coordinator" or e-zine editor. Again, this is a great way to network with other writers and build a support network. Participate on group blogs with other writers; check out:
http://www.absolutewrite.com/forums/,
http://wordservewatercooler.com/ and
avalonauthors.blogspot.com/.

Fire Starter # 34-Join a reader/author reviews site

$ For Free!

Sites like **www.Goodreads.com** or **www.Shelfari.com** allow authors and readers to post plot summaries and reviews of books they've written or read, and then rank them on a sliding scale. By joining early, and writing reviews for other authors, you can cultivate relationships that may pay off with reviews of your own books once published.
Shelfari allows members to migrate their information from their Amazon account, so you don't have to type in every book.

Fire Starter # 35-Add factoids and extras to Shelfari

Shelfari lets readers add "book factoids" to the "Book Extras" section located in the back of Kindle eBooks. In this way, you can add a level of interactivity between you and your readers that can be utilized for games and contests. Remember, reader engagement with interactive features drives better results than passive advertising.

Stoke Your Book For Success With Product & Key Word Placement:

Stoke your book for success by pre-loading it to attract and retain reader interest, specifically in your target segment. Seed your book with creative elements that can be used as promotional tools during your marketing campaign. Stoking your book for success means ensuring you have included creative elements in the book that are relevant to your audience and more importantly, can later be used to promote the book. Those elements may be there already, or you may need to go back and add them. So before you lock and load the book, and before you go to print, think about how you might insert some creative elements to help promote your book.

Fire Starter # 36-Stoke your book for promotional contests

Everyone loves a contest. And YOU should love the contest that requires folks to read your book to get the information they need to win. Develop a contest where the reader must find the five incorrect historical references to win a prize, for example. Of course, you will need to seed your book with five incorrect historical references. Alternatively, run a contest to find the five lines from famous classic stories (that are no longer under copyright). What about inserting a drinking game right into the book? That's a crazy idea! It's just crazy enough to work.

Fire Starter # 37-Seed your book with products, accessories, famous places and other items that you can tie to promotional campaigns during the launch

Go back through your book and see what you have to work with. If you don't have some elements that you can leverage, strongly consider a small re-write to seed your book with a few things that will help you create a buzz during launch. Be creative! Here are some ideas to get you started.

1. Have a main character be obsessed and therefore always eating popular snack/food items like Oreo cookies or Funyuns. Serve Oreos at every book signing or other events. Bonus: see if you can get the company to co-market.

2. Perhaps your main character has a unique tattoo or body art? To see how they created intrigue with Jack's tattoos in the television series "Lost," check out: http://lostpedia.wikia.com/wiki/Jack's_tattoos. Create fake tattoos to match your characters and wear them at all events. Give away matching fake tattoos on your Web site. Alternatively, run a contest for anyone having a tattoo similar to your character's tattoo. Give a prize for the one that's closest.

This Worked For: San Francisco restaurant Casa Sanchez. Several years ago, the restaurant won a best marketing campaign award (voted by Forbes magazine) for offering free tacos for life to anyone sporting a Casa Sanchez tattoo. They exchanged commitment for commitment!

3. Perhaps a main character has a special walking cane or hat or other prop/article of clothing that is part of his/her or her character (think Harry Potter's glasses). Use as a prop or give away during promotional events for the book.
4. Perhaps a character carries around/uses tarot cards; make a special deck and give away on your Website or tie them into a contest.
5. Perhaps one of your characters has a "signature" graphic tee-with a statement on it-that he/she wears all the time; the statement should be unique and relevant to your book. Create an unusual tee and give away or use as a promotional item.
6. We realize that book titles are a very personal thing for authors. However, if you are not married to your title, re-evaluate and see if it's something you can work with from a promotional perspective.

Remember, you are trying to create a flame - a buzz around your book - you need some material to work with. Furthermore, research suggests that titles are often the **one thing** that attracts readers and causes them to pick up your book in the first place. No surprise there.

This Worked For: There are lots of examples of catchy titles that became part of the promotion buzz. Here are some examples from Goodreads; to check out, the complete list of "Best Book Titles" go to http://www.goodreads.com/list/show/276.Best_Book_Titles *The Hollow Chocolate Bunnies of the Apocalypse*-for this title, we would hand out hollow chocolate bunnies at promotional events...duh. *Pride and Prejudice and* Zombies -everyone knows that zombies are big attention grabbers, and this title is loaded with possibilities. For example, how about characters from P & P, but in zombie form - moaning and lunging at visitors at book launch events?! *I Was Told There'd Be Cake*-shame on them if they didn't have cake at the book launch.

Fire Starter # 38-Seed your book with famous places (or not so famous) and leverage THEIR creative marketing campaigns,

For example, have a character frequent the "Heart Attack Grill" where he orders "Triple Bypass Burgers" daily served up by half naked nurses (no kidding, this is a real place). Again, see if you can get some co-promotion interest from the restaurant/city/town etc. Could they, would they, sell your book in the restaurant? Remind them what "Twilight" did for Forks.

Another example: have a character own a Blendtec ™ blender. Throughout the book, the character frequently tests the limits of the blender by putting different things in it-like expensive electronics. This way, you are playing off the now-famous Blendtec campaign (see Antic Advertising section for more on this campaign). Make sure you acknowledge a trademark where appropriate. Tie a promotion with a You Tube video of the various things being blended from the book.

And what if your setting is the fictional town of Nutter Hill? Why not create a Website dedicated to this imaginary place that offers visitors a view of life in Nutter Hill. Make up facts about the town and create characters that are not in the book like a Mayor and the local barber. Don't forget to include a map of some of the hot spots for tourists.

Fire Starter # 39-Create a "best of" list and populate on Websites, Twitter, etc.

Do you have a character in the book who loves to throw out snappy zingers like the House character on the popular television series? House went off the air recently so fans made a "best of" House video with him spewing some of his best insults. This seems like a good idea to promote a book.

Light A Fire With Email: Start creating your email list of likely targets

In this chapter, we're going to talk about creating an email list of potential buyers. You need to start creating this list as soon as possible. People in your book-marketing, email list should include those you feel might buy your book when it's ready to launch. However, you don't have to wait until your book is ready to launch to reach out to your prospects and start developing relationships through email. You can offer other types of content to get folks engaged with you before your book goes to market. In a later chapter, we will cover additional email marketing strategies you can use once your book launches.

First, however, let's talk about obtaining value from the email list! In these days of flashy-sparkly media rich pitches and social networking sites, using plain-vanilla email may seem outdated and well, boring. Also, you may have heard digital marketing experts make dire predictions like "email will be dead in the next five years." Well, in today's rapidly changing world, it may, in fact, be long-gone in five years; however, today, email is alive and well and should be a central component of your online marketing campaign.

Email marketing should, however, be an integrated part of your marketing mix and not an isolated effort. As we have said previously in this book, it's important that all your digital marketing sites, and tools be integrated as much as possible.

Email marketing is still a good investment of your time for the following reasons:

1. Email is still the most widely used form of Internet communications, especially among the 20+ age population. Now, if you are directly targeting young adults and teens with your marketing messages, then you could afford to disregard email in your mix and focus perhaps more on mobile strategies;

2. It can play many roles in your campaign: you can share valuable information quickly and cheaply building credibility as an "expert" in your field, and it's still the best way to cultivate relationships with new customers and fans. You can drive prospects to your Web site to close the sale, or build excitement over time for a book launch with a drip campaign (we discuss this concept in more detail later in the book);

3. Most importantly, email marketing allows you to develop highly targeted messages and deliver them to customers who have already expressed interest in you or your book. You can deliver customized, personal, timely and relevant messages, which will increase response rates. For example, if you want to send one message to all the people, you met at a school book signing and a different message to those you met at a book fair, you can do so. You can run a promotion with email subscribers in a specific state or county and send different messages to various groups of based on age or gender. You can't do this as easily if you are broadcasting messages on social media sites as these sites are not as personal and messages get lost in all the clutter. The more personal and relevant the marketing message, the better chance you have of the prospect responding to your campaign;

4. Because you can "get personal" in email, it's the best way to build new relationships and nurture and reward existing relationships with

your fans. Use email to thank your readers for their business, wish them a happy birthday and ask for their feedback;

5. You can also build viral campaigns effectively by including social media "share" buttons in your email;

6. Email marketing improves conversion rates. Converting visitors to your Website into customers requires a few more "impressions" or touches. In other words, first-time visitors to your site usually don't buy anything. Research has shown that prospects must receive multiple marketing messages before they are convinced to purchase. This is where email marketing comes in. It allows you to stay in touch with people who visit your Website and ping them with additional marketing messages until they are ready to buy;

7. And did we say, it's still one of the most inexpensive marketing tools out there?

Okay, we've made our case for email marketing. Hopefully, you are convinced. Let's talk about some email marketing basics.

Note for additional email marketing tips visit
http://emailmarketing.comm100.com/email-marketing-tutorial/email-marketing-tips.aspx

As we mentioned above, the first step in email marketing is to develop your database of quality email subscribers. Remember, email marketing allows you to deliver highly customized messages directly to people who have expressed interest in you or your book. If you build your email database the right way, your email list includes people who have given you permission to send them an email. This is called "opt in" or "permission" marketing and is email marketing best practice. People who have "opted in" to receive your communications are more likely to read your emails versus people who get your emails from out of the blue. Opt in email marketing is the strategy we recommend.

The other way to build your email marketing database is to buy email lists. We do not recommend this strategy. Getting an unsolicited email is considered "spam" by many and is typically not appreciated. Sending emails to people who have indicated they want to hear from you is very effective. These are the highest quality leads you can ever hope to gain.

When should you buy an email list? When you can buy a targeted list and can provide free, useful content to the members of that list, you will entice them to opt-in for later mailings. An example of this would be a writer of non-fiction books for second graders who purchases an email list of second-grade teachers, and in the first email them a free lesson plan based on the content of one of the books. Building a quality list and maintaining it takes time and energy but as many successful authors have discovered, it's worth it. Here are some tips to building your email marketing database:

Fire Starter # 40-Create a compelling value proposition

First, create a compelling reason for people to want to join your email list and receive email from you. In marketing, we call this your "value proposition." This could be a newsletter they get once a month with updates on events and happenings (book signings), and chock-full of helpful cooking tips (if you are selling a cookbook). Alternatively, you could offer original content and access to exclusive resources.

This Worked For: Dave Balch, author of *Cancer for Two*, developed a series of "Coping Quickies" which are tips for coping with cancer or coping as a caregiver of someone with cancer. Dave has partnered with health care companies to deliver the tips as a value-added benefit to members and customers.

Fire Starter # 41- Create incentives and hold a contest.

Provide incentives for people to sign up. Run a contest; if they sign up for your email list, their name will be entered into a raffle to win a free book or other related merchandise. Use lottery tickets* as incentives; market your giveaway as a chance to "win a million dollars" (or whatever the grand prize is in your area) for every sign up received during a particular time period. Or, if they join your email list, you will send them discount coupons for your books (works well if you are writing a series). Even better, develop exclusive offers or content just for your email list subscribers. Offer pre-order and preview opportunities (the chance to preview selected chapters of your next book first and receive signed copies) or promise to send them additional content that is not in the book.

* **Warning:** be cognizant of state and federal laws for raffles and prize drawings.

Fire Starter # 42-Mine your social network and collect email addresses wherever you go.

Next, start collecting email addresses wherever you are and wherever you go. For starters, mine your current social network, including your email box and your Facebook page. Offer plenty of opportunities to "join my email list" on your Website and social media sites. If you are offering a newsletter as your carrot to get their email address, make sure to include samples or back issues on your Web site for them to review.

Capture email addresses at every event/book fair/book signing, etc. Anytime you are at an event, plan to capture email addresses face-face. While you are networking, ask people if you can follow up with them via email to let them know when your book (or next book) will be available.

Fire Starter # 43- Develop a "Refer a Friend" program

Another great way to build your list over time is to ask your loyal fans (once you have them) to refer a friend to your email list. You can offer your fans a "refer a friend" reward.

Don't forget to develop a un-subscribe feature for your email list or newsletter. Offer easy-to-find un-subscribe links on your Web site so people can easily un-subscribe to your mailing list. This is email marketing best practice and highly recommended. It doesn't have to be an automated system. You can simply ask them to send you an email if they would like to un-subscribe to your mailing list. To learn how to use your list to market your book and develop long-term relationships with prospects, check out the chapter called *"Keep Your Fires Blazing Using Email and Twitter."*

PART TWO: FAN THE FLAMES IN THE FOUR-MONTH COUNT-DOWN TO YOUR BOOK'S PUB DAY

Get Your Book Sales Crackling with eBooks:

It's probably a universal truth that there's not an author in the world who hasn't lusted after a printed book. Whether it's the weight of the book in the hands, the gold tipping at the ends, or the rustle of the pages, they call to us from their perch on the bookshelf, "pick me up; make me yours!" So it's only natural that we want our own work in print as well.

However, in this changing world, there are many authors choosing eBook format over print and making a good living at it. Presently, Amazon sells about six eBooks for every ten printed books. Suffice it to say, the eBook market is growing in leaps and bounds. If you choose not to make an eBook version of your book, you run the risk of missing out on a growing segment of the market.

So, how do you make your book an eBook? Well, if you are traditionally published, find out if your publisher has your digital rights (have a lawyer or agent look at your contract) contract), if they do, ask them to publish it as an eBook. If they do have your rights but decline to publish it as an eBook, ask if you can buy those rights back for a nominal sum. If they don't have your rights, this means you have your rights, so read on!

There are a variety of paths you can take to publish your book as an eBook. You can choose your selling venues and format it yourself (use coding software to lighten your load); you can let Google or Amazon do it for you, or you can pay the professionals. The first step is to decide where you will be selling it.

The major players for eBook sales are presently Amazon with Kindle books, Apple with its iBook store, Barnes & Noble with the Nook, and Google with the Nexus tablet. Each has its own formatting requirements, and of course; they all differ. If you decide to sell in more than one venue, you may wish to pay a professional to code it for you. Read more about this below. However, if you are starting out small, and decide to concentrate on the pack leader, Amazon, then you can actually do it yourself and save some money.

Code it Yourself

$ Between Free to Low Cost.

Amazon uses its own format for Kindle books called AZW. It's similar to HTML, but with different tagging. Don't worry. You don't have to be an HTML or AZW coding expert to prep your book to be an eBook, and doing it yourself costs nothing but your time.

Here are free resources for learning enough code to get your eBook on Amazon and Kindle:

https://kdp.amazon.com/self-publishing/help?topicId=A17W8UM0MMSQX6

http://www.amazon.com/dp/B007URVZJ6

Mac users go here: https://kdp.amazon.com/self-publishing/help?topicId=A2AOXJXY43GME3.

Use Coding Software to Lighten Your Load

$ Between Free to Low Cost.

If the thought of self-coding your book seems daunting, you can take a short cut by using software. Check out Calibre at http://calibre-eBook.com/, or Mobipocket eBook Creator at http://www.mobipocket.com/en/downloadsoft/productdetailscreator.asp for two free programs. Note that Mobipocket Creator can convert your book from a Word document to AZW, while both programs allow conversion to HTML. Using Mobipocket Creator is supposed to be easy; just save your doc as "Webpage, filtered," then upload to Mobi and the program should convert.

*Warning; See Tip below.

Another easy way to produce a coded eBook is to use Scrivener to code your book for you. Scrivener is a popular writing program for novelists and screen play writers that can be found at www.literatureandlatte.com. For $49.99 you get a great writing tool and the ability to export your work (using the Compile button) in a variety of formats, including rich text format (rtf), Kindle ready (mobi), eBook (epub), Web page ready (html), and Adobe (pdf). Already have Scrivener? Go to "File" scroll down to "Compile,'" choose your "Format for" as either custom or Novel Ready, and then choose your "Compile as" to pick your end product output.

HOT TIP* Always preview your manuscript on an audience ready device (such as Nook, Kindle or Kindle for PC/Mac) if possible before uploading to your selling venue (more on that below) BEFORE you go live with your publication. If you have fancy formatting or want to include illustrations you may need to add coding to your outputted document.

Hire the Experts

$$-$$$ Moderate to Major Bucks!

If you have decided to sell at multiple venues, or if you have a book that requires a lot of special formatting or includes a lot of images, you might consider hiring an expert. The booming eBook market has resulted in a growing number of coding and formatting companies. Some charge per word, while others charge per project. Check out a few of them here: https://kdp.amazon.com/self-publishing/help?topicId=A3RRQXI478DDG7.

Note: even though these are listed on the Amazon Web site, most convert for Amazon, Smashwords and Google sales. Cost will vary depending on the length of your book, the number of versions you need for different forums and the amount of formatting involved.

Fire Starter # 44-Make your sales snap by using Google to sell your eBooks

With the Google Nexus tablet (a seven inch multimedia tablet running Android), Google is taking on the Kindle. To support its tablet with content, Google launched Google Play in the spring 2012. The homepage for Google Play is located here: https://play.google.com/store?hl=en&tab=88.

The top of the screen lists the content categories with "My Books" being the second one over from the left. If you click through on My Books, it takes you to a page with explanatory content at the top. Beneath this you scroll through several categories, like "New York Times Best Seller," and "Top Free" before you get to the "Categories" list. At the date of the last edit for this page of this book, there were not a lot of books listed in Google Play - yet. Since there are no numbers posted anywhere that indicate the quantity of books being sold, we had to click through categories to get a feel for it. To give you an example of how shallow the pool was at that time, Young Adult Books were listed as a sub-category under "Children's Books" and the total number in the store was 102. By the time this book makes it to market, these numbers will likely change however, this does indicate an opportunity for the savvy eBook author to get their book noticed before the site gets crowded.

To sell books on Google Play, you have to be a member of the Google Book Partners Program. Check the program out here: http://support.google.com/books/partner/bin/static.py?hl=en&page=guide.cs&guide=1346912&topic=1346917. Google Play charges 52% royalty based on a retail price you set. They require submitted books to be in pdf or ePub format.

Fire Starter # 45-Let Amazon Kindle Direct Publishing fire your eBook sales.

$ Free to Little Cost!

Once you have a Kindle ready book, it's easy and FREE to upload it to the Kindle Book market place at Amazon. Kindle Direct Publishing (KDP) offers as much as a 70% royalty for placing your book in markets where they are available for purchase on Kindle devices and Kindle apps for iPad, iPhone, iPod touch, PC, Mac, BlackBerry, and Android-based devices. Go to https://kdp.amazon.com/self-publishing/signin for more information.

KDP also offers a program called "KDP Select" where if you sell your book exclusively through Amazon for a set period of time and allow it to be made available through Amazon's lending library (for Amazon Prime members), you can share, based on the number of times your book is borrowed during the month, from a fund set aside for this purpose. You also get 5 days per each 90 day period during which you can offer your book for free. Some authors report bumps in sales, and higher sales ranks, when they use these free days. See https://kdp.amazon.com/self-publishing/KDPSelect for more information.

Fire Starter # 46-Develop marketing strategies to support your FREE Days

While posting your eBook to Kindle is **FREE,** you can choose to incur costs in the marketing campaigns you design to support your free days. You might want to do this to get the best "bump" in sales. There are paid services that promise to do this, but you can also do things that are free. For example, you can create a Pinterest board about your free book event, announce your free days as an "Event" on Face Book, and line-up some blog interviews.

For more on using KDP and Select, see *Use Fire Starters to Flame Your Book Sales* in Part Three.

Light A Fire With Your Own Media Kit

$ From Inexpensive to $$$ Major Bucks!

A media kit or press kit is a set of promotional materials and information developed to send to members of the media to introduce yourself and build awareness and buzz about your book. We suggest, however, that you think in broader terms when you think about developing a media kit. You should consider this your "marketing tool kit" as the items and information in this kit can also be sent to potential partners, influential bloggers, reviewers and even readers.

Many authors are now building online media pages and directing interested parties and media types to these pages. However, if you have the time and money, we believe it's still a good investment to develop a few printed materials and giveaways that can be snail mailed or dropped off with reporters and other key influencers. In this day of the Internet and emails, sending a package in the mail with goodies included, just may be the **thing** that gets you noticed.

The main purpose of your media/marketing kit is to inspire someone to want to learn more about you and your book. If you are targeting the media, your kit needs to suggest story ideas; more on that concept later. Also, media kits can be important for opening doors; so while you may not get a reporter to cover your book launch, a media kit can help you get speaking engagements and other opportunities that could eventually lead to book sales.

Your media/marketing kit should include the following elements: press release, author bio with picture, giveaways, signed books for reviewers, business cards, book-related goodies for reader incentives and contests. Your bio should include a "wall of fame" if you're lucky enough to have received positive reviews or had featured articles written about your book.

Don't forget, reporters and other influencers are overloaded with information so you want to try to stand out and be remembered. In the realm of media kits, you have an advantage. Use your creative talents to make your pitch interesting enough to break through the clutter. That's half the battle.

When should you start creating your media kit? The answer: At least four months before your book launch if possible. It's important to have some tools in your kit ready to go when you launch your book so you can immediately respond to any inquiries.

The cost of media kits will vary significantly depending on whether or not you plan to mail kits or just direct reporters to an online kit. If you plan to send promotional items like pens or coffee mugs, and if you include a signed copy of your book when you send out a press release to a reporter or reviewer, the kit can get pricey. For a kit with printed materials and giveaways, the cost can be anywhere from $20.00 to $1,000.00 or more per kit.

Where to pitch?

Remember, in order to create a blaze, you need to light many flames so our advice is to pitch everywhere you can. Here are some ideas of where to pitch your story.

Fire Starter # 47-Pitch to free and paid services

Make sure and pitch to free and paid online sites if you can afford it. Targeting both will give you a better chance at being heard. Paid options include PRNewswire, **PRWeb** and **PitchEngine**. For a less-expensive route, check out **free** Press Release and PR Log.

Fire Starter # 48-Leverage sites like "Help a Reporter Out"

Pitch to sites like "Help a Reporter Out" which connects journalists to experts and story ideas. HARO allows reporters to find sources or "subject matter experts" using an online query system. Reporters may be looking for a book to review, or they may be looking for a subject matter expert on a topic they are covering like obesity or depression in teens. This is a good strategy for non-fiction writers.

Additional Resources
To learn more about creating a media kit, check out these online resources:
http://www.ehow.com/how_2050389_create-media-kit.html

Press Releases

There is a healthy debate as to whether or not sending press releases to the media, either directly or through online distribution sites, is a waste of time for a book launch, unless of course you are J. K. Rowling about to go live with the next installment of Harry Potter. We agree; it's not going to be easy getting the media, either local or national, to cover your launch. However, one could argue; it's still worth your time to send out press releases announcing your new book on-line to increase your visibility. It's important for you to be visible on the Web as most people search on-line for products and services or things that interest them.

On-line press releases may rank high in search engines. So, pitching could contribute to your overall on-line presence and visibility and the speed at which your potential customers can find you. And remember, all your online marketing efforts should tie together and drive each other. So don't forget to include links to your Web site in your press release.

Furthermore, if you book launch does get some coverage by the media, it's a relatively cheap form of advertising and well worth the effort. So, whether you decide to pitch to the national media directly or distribute to free and paid sites online, let's look at how to light a fire with a press release:
1. Ideally whenever you send out a press release, it should include other elements of your media kit, like publishing information on the book, photos from the book, and of you the author, your bio and a cover letter.
2. The release itself should attempt to imitate either a news story or a book review.
3. In order to get picked up by mainstream media, you need to: a) have a newsworthy story to report, or one with a significant hook,

and b) contact individual media outlets, reach out to the reporter or editor who might be interested in your story, and submit the story to them directly. However, to light a fire online or off, you need a hook. So the first step is to create a press release with a hook. Here are some tips:

Fire Starter # 49-Create a headline with a hook

Make sure your headline has a hook; your headline must be written to grab the attention of the reader. If the headline doesn't grab them, reporters generally won't bother reading the rest of the press release. But don't go crazy. If you write a headline like, "Incredible new book solves the world's problems," the reporter/editor will most likely toss your release out. However, if you write something interesting and relevant like, "Survey shows that Americans are getting fat from watching TV" the reporter might see relevance for his audience.

Fire Starter # 50-Create a story with a bigger hook

Obviously, the "story" you create in the release needs a hook as well. If it's a small-town paper, they are looking for news with a local slant. So if you want them to cover your book launch, especially if you are self-published, you need to find a local angle. Of course, if you are pitching in the city you grew up in, that will help.

So what can you do to get them to cover your story? Come up with a charitable angle – donate 10 percent of your book sales to a local charity during a certain month. Alternatively, donate books to libraries or schools and promote reading literacy in underprivileged areas of town.

Create a publicity stunt or local Antic Advertising event: for a romance novel targeted at 30+ women, hire local actors to act out scenes in shopping centers. Make sure to include kissing scenes. Or, if you wrote a book about Lincoln, host a President Lincoln look-alike contest.

Connect your book to a national news story or trend. For example, talk about how your book is going to save the nation from the ills of reality television.

Tell YOUR story; but only if you can create an interesting or relevant angle; talk about overcoming obstacles to write the book as a single mother, talk about the research you did to get into the characters' heads (trip to Lebanon, etc.) Include lists with your press release if possible: The media loves a sound bite with a story that can easily be presented with bullets. So make it easy for them. Include the "Best of" list or a list like "Six ways to lose a lover."

Think about how you can glean a list out of your content. Here are some real-life examples: "Six Best Places To Retire on a Budget"; "Six tools no Web site developer should be without" If it's a romance novel, and the hero woes the heroine away from someone else, then how about "Ten ways to win over a girl who is dating someone else."

Study the masters! *Cracked* magazine features 3-6 new stories each day with "Best of," "Top of" type stories. Read them to see how they hook their audience. Here are some other great on-line resources that tell you just how to go about writing and pitching a press release on-line.
http://www.theBookdesigner.com/2011/03/how-to-write-a-press-release-a-mini-tutorial/

Fire Starter # 51-Create an on-line media kit

An on-line media kit is really just a page on your Web site dedicated to the media and designed to help people help you get the word out. It's the on-line place where you will send reporters, bloggers, reviewers and potential partners. This page shouldn't be about selling books, however; don't send reporters to pages on your site where you are making offers and trying to sell.

This page should include all the information in your media kit mentioned above: contact information, bio, press release, reviews. It should also include the basic content we mention above for your

Web site like video trailers, calendar of upcoming events like book signings, links to all your social media pages and author pages on other sites like Amazon.

Other content to consider that is especially important to your media page includes:

Fire Starter # 52-Make it easy with Talking Points

Summarize your bio, press release and book into sound bites or talking points. This gives the media a summary of your content in a format they prefer so they don't have to create their own. Also, they probably won't read your book so don't make them search for the major themes or what is unique and special about your work.

Fire Starter # 53-Use FAQ's and mock interviews

Develop mock interview questions or FAQ's (frequently asked questions); again, make it very easy for a reporter or anyone who wants to help you sell your book or schedule you for a speaking engagement. Create mock questions and answers that directly hit the key points you want to make about your book. Remember, it's important to find a hook. Reporters will be interested in content that help people solve a problem or get closer to their goals (lose weight, eat healthier, take more time with my family or reduce stress).

Try to communicate a real benefit of your book and make sure to remain relevant by relating to world events or trends if possible. For example, if the economy is on everyone's mind (like it is now), then relate your book launch to the economic crises. Be creative. Even if your book is pure entertainment, you can link it to the bad economy; "In this time of worry and stress, don't we all need a blissful release? Don't we all want to immerse ourselves into a fantasy world and forget about the real world, if only for a few hours?" Furthermore, don't forget to answer the question "why should I read/buy this book?" Your response could start with "this book is good for anyone who wants to…...

This Worked For: For a great example of an author who uses the technique above, check out Andy Andrews's media page at http://www.andyandrews.com/ms/the-final-summit/Andrews-The_Final_Summit-MediaKit.pdf

Fire Starter # 54-Offer interesting/interactive features

Leverage interactive features like virtual tours to create interest. Is there something unique about your writing style or where you get your inspiration? Create a virtual tour (video) of the places you get inspiration or your work space highlighting your writing process.

Fire Starter # 55-Add fire starting giveaways and incentives to your media/marketing kit

Use companies like Vistaprint (online provider of customized promotional products) or GOpromos.com to develop giveaways for the media or book reviewers. You can also use these items as contest prizes and other goodies for your fans. Find a favorite quote from your book and print it on a tee shirt for a give-away or create bookmarks with your book cover and Web site address.

Make up cards with a calendar printed on them and circle important dates. Put contact information and your Web site address on one side with a picture of your cover on the other side.

Develop book-related theme giveaways. Get creative.

This Worked For: Opus Event Marketing Company allegedly sent out tiny tubs of Play-Doh as part of their "Let's Play in New York" campaign, which was meant to announce the opening of its new office. Total cost was reported at $300. If your book is a fantasy about vampires, send cheap Halloween vampire teeth and vampire blood with your press release to local reporters and other key influencers.

Fire Starter # 56 -Offer book club host incentives

Create book club host incentives for anyone who wants to host a book club event. Give away promotional items to your book club hosts. This is similar to the Pampered Chef or jewelry companies that provide "gifts" to people who host parties to sell their products. Why couldn't you do this for the host of a book club party where your book is reviewed?

This Worked For: Check out this offer page by Gary Vaynerchuk to get ideas for volume incentives: http://crushitbook.com/crush-it-the-experience/

Light A Fire With Reviews

Reviews have become an essential marketing tool for selling books online. They can be shared in many different marketing channels; displayed on your Website, shared on all your social media outposts, included as part of your email campaigns or email signature. As we mentioned before, young adults rely heavily on reviews and recommendations from friends and family. If you shop on-line, you know that reviews are available for almost any product or service, so they have essentially become an integral part of the on-line shopping experience, especially on Amazon.

When it comes to how to obtain reviews, there are as many opinions as there are options. You can obtain reviews through a more organic approach asking family, friends, fans and visitors to your Web site/Amazon page to "pretty please" post a review. These reviews have the ring of truth because while they may be solicited, you are not paying for them. Alternatively, you can pay for reviews.

Some authors find fault in paid-for reviews, but others argue that traditional publishers have been leveraging this practice since the beginning of time in the form of "blurbs," and even respected reviewers, like Kirkusreviews.com, will review any book for a price. You must do the research and form your own opinions about paid-for reviews, but keep in mind, reviews can be an important part of your marketing mix, and we encourage you to investigate the options.

It's a crowded market out there, and positive reviews can help you stand out from the masses. Obviously, quality reviews from honest, unbiased sources are ideal whether they are paid for or not.

Submit to Major Reviewers Requiring at Least a 12-Week Window

$$$ Major Bucks!

If you are agented/pubbed, be sure to have the submission to these reviewers negotiated into your contract. Ask your publisher for their submission list, and if there is a reviewer not on it that you would like to hear from, ask for their inclusion. If your publisher refuses, ask for the right to submit on your own. Several of the more traditional reviewers are setting up divisions to deal with self-pubbed and Indie-pubbed. If you fall in these categories, you can submit to:

1. Kirkus: Reviewer of books since 1933. Kirkusreviews.com. They take 9 weeks to return Indie reviews and charge $425.00, or you can pay $575.00 to have your review returned in 6 weeks. Go to: www.kirkususreviews.com/indie/about/. As per their Web site, a reviewer reads the complete book and offers a 250 word to 350 word review. The review is sent to you via email and you may use it as you wish. If good, make sure to publish it for **FREE** at www.kirkusreviews.com. You can also add it to the cover of your book, your Web site and other promotional pieces. For non-indie reviews go to www.kirkusreviews.com.

2. Publisher's Weekly: Self-published authors can register to have their book listed in a seasonal supplement they bind into issues of Publisher's Weekly. This includes the mirror digital and online editions. The cost for both print and eBooks is $149.00, and includes a six-month subscription to Publisher's Weekly. If you are a current subscriber, you get one free listing. Since a digital one-year subscription is $209.00, this means you get the subscription for only $59.00 more than the cost of the book listing. Publisher's Weekly states on its Web site that they select 25% of the submitted self-

published listings for a full review. See:
http://www.publishersweekly.com/pw/corp/diy-reg-Instructions.html.

For a fairly comprehensive list of major and significant reviewing journals and magazines, see: http://www.complete-review.com/links/links.html.

Submit for Free Reviews:

$ - The Only Cost is Your Time

Submit to Newspapers Requiring a 6-12 Week Window:
Be sure and submit to your hometown and local newspapers. You may also want to submit to one or more of the larger markets. For a comprehensive contact list, see:
http://www.bookmarket.com/newspapers.htm.

Fire Starter # 57-Submit a review of someone else's work for soft sale exposure

The following review sites encourage readers to submit reviews, and allow the reviewer to tag his or her Web site and pubs for exposure. This is an excellent way to build awareness for your book for basically **FREE** and soft sell. We encourage you to do as many of these as you can.

http://thebooxreview.com/reviews.htm

http://www.myshelf.com/aboutus/want_reviewers.htm

http://www.midwestbookreview.com/revinfo.htm

To be even more strategic, write and post reviews of books like *yours* on Amazon or other sites. Soft-sell your book by starting each of your reviews with a tag like, "As the author of (your book title) I've written on a similar subject, and must say …" Be authentic of course but keep your critical commentary to a minimum. This will prevent your review from being seen by others as a snarky attempt to discredit your competition. Also, people tend to read more than one book on a subject they are interested in, so your review can be your audition to make your book their next acquisition.

Post Publication Day Reviews:

A lot of post-publication reviewers will review books published within the current calendar year. This puts a squeeze on those with a late in the year pub date. Review each site for their deadlines and requirements.

$ Free Post Publication Review Services:

http://thekindleBookreview.blogspot.com/p/get-reviewed-2.html- reviews indie pubbed books. Contact one reviewer from their staff, including in your query a brief synopsis, cover art, the author's name, the title of the book, and a link to your book in the Amazon Kindle store.

MyShelf- http://www.myshelf.com/aboutus/request.htm - this site requires books to be available on Amazon and is currently only taking 2013 titles.

http://www.bookpleasures.com/Web sitepublisher/categories/Book-Review-Submission-Guidelines/ - this site requires that your book be listed and for sale on Amazon at the time, you submit your request for review. Reviews take 1-4 months. You can request a "priority review" for $119.00; you will receive your "editorial" review within 15 business days of payment and submission. See: http://www.bookpleasures.com/Web sitepublisher/pages/Do-You-Need-A-Quick-Review-Of-Your-Book%3F.html'

The Midwest Book Review at http://www.midwestbookreview.com/get_rev.htm gives priority consideration to small publishers, self-published authors, academic presses and specialty publishers. They require two finished copies of the book, a cover letter and a publicity release or media kit to submit a book for review – see how that media kit can come in handy!

Amazon lists its top 1000 (yes, that's one thousand!) reviewers at: http://www.amazon.com/review/top-reviewers. Contact a few hundred of these and you're bound to entice one or two to do reviews. Note: to have your book reviewed by an Amazon Top Reviewer, your book must be sold through Amazon. Also, these reviewers are not Amazon employees and apparently receive no compensation for their reviews. You can click on their names to read about their interests and obtain their email address if they have provided one, but whether they will review your work is entirely up to them.

Additional Resources-Other Independent Reviewers:

http://www.theindieview.com/indie-reviewers/

http://www.midwestbookreview.com/links/othr_rev.htm

http://www.stepbystepselfpublishing.net/reviewer-list.html

http://pippajay.blogspot.com/p/book-reviewers-list.html

http://www.onlinecollege.org/2009/09/15/100-best-blogs-for-book-reviews/

http://www.bookreviewblogs.com/blog-list/all/top

Paid for Review Services:
$$-$$$ -Between Moderate and Major Bucks

http://www.theBookplex.com/authors.html?gclid=CJ6J7Nu3n7ECF WyHtgodhBqTYw. Takes approximately three to four weeks to provide reviews. Reviews cost $45.00 for five or $85.00 for ten. See also www.bookpleasures.com above.

Light a Fire With Crowd Funding: Use other people's money to jump-start your sales!

Have you been looking at some of those $$ and $$$ signs and feeling a little green envy? Want to take your marketing up a level but don't have the budget? Crowd funding may be the answer. This funding strategy tap into a grassroots approach to obtaining funds for creative projects, and with big institutions like music labels and publishing companies on the decline, creatives need new sources of funding to get projects off the ground.

Crowd funding, or crowd financing organizations bring creators together with supporters to provide funding for the completion of a creative project. Simply put, people use crowd funding services/sites to solicit small donations from many different supporters over the Internet.

Funding is usually donation based in that supporters do not obtain any rights to the projects they support. Instead, funding is typically offered at staggered levels in exchange for some version of the creative project with increasing incentives, such as swag, author dedications, meetings and enhanced editions. Note that most crowd funding platforms require the donation seeker to develop their own incentive levels, and the products (T-shirts, mugs, magnets) that accompany them.

The creator is also required to perform all support services associated with these incentives, such as packaging and shipping. There are a few, though, that have a number of incentives available at the touch of the button. These are profit centers for these platforms. However, they take most of the hassle out of incentive management. Payment for the incentives is taken out of the creator/donation seeker's donations along with the crowd funding platform fees and credit card processing fees.

Important* Some crowdfunding platforms require the creator to obtain donations totaling the entire budget specified for the project in order to receive any money, while others permit the creator to keep all donations even if the project goal is not reached.

So why would total strangers donate money to help you complete or market your new book? There are many reasons, including a desire to help the "little guy" achieve the American Dream and to have a say in what products, films, books, etc. make it to market. Most crowd funding organizations require creators to describe their project, with detail about their plan for completing it, including a completion date, and to provide a budget showing how the sponsors' money will be spent. Some sites also strongly suggest creators provide a short video explaining all the above in a personal plea for support.

Typically, a crowd funding organization will require the creator to identify a charge card, bank account or PayPal account to accept supporters' payments. While there are a few that charge no fee, most are commission based, charging a fee based on the total money transferred from the supporters to the creators. Finally, some do not allow partial funding. This means if a project fails to make budget, the supporters do not get charged and no money transfers.

Crowd funding is an excellent opportunity for authors who have a creative marketing campaign in mind and need some money to pull it off. For example, to market this book, we decided to offer authors the opportunity to submit their work to us and we had incentives, like posters, mugs, bookmarks, and book evaluations. Another example that would attract attention of the high tech crowd is to create a game, app, or other interactive tool based on your book. See the chapter on *Gamification* for ideas.

In budgeting for a crowd funding project, make sure to include all costs of providing supporter incentives, including production, shipping, organizational commission charges and credit card or

PayPal charges. At the same time, don't include too much padding as most crowd funding sites allow supporters to donate within your campaign period even after you've met your budget goals.

Finally, build enough time in your incentive delivery schedule to enable you to delay ordering pledge fulfillment items (bookmarks, magnets, coffee mugs and other swag) until you are sure your project will make budget.

Here are some crowd funding organizations that support written works or projects associated with written works:

FUNDLY, www.fundly.com. "Raise money for anything." Fundly allows you to manage your campaign on the go with a free app. It also permits donors to view campaigns and donate to campaigns via the app. The Fundly Website states that it is integrated with Facebook so that your campaign activity can be broadcast on Facebook. In addition, it lets you import your email contacts. Fundly also integrates product sales for incentives by offering you access to T-shirts, mugs, magnets, bags, iPhone cases and other items. Once you chose to incentivize a giving level, the cost of the items is taken out of the donation. Fundly also sends the donor his incentive.

Fees and Payments: Fundly processes payments through WePay. Partial funding is permitted, and payments are processed and available within 48 hours of donation. Fundly deducts 4.9% in fees and another 3% in credit card processing fees for a total of 7.9% from each donation.

FUNDRAZR, www.fundrazr.com. "Raise money for what matters to you." It claims to have built-in sharing features to integrate your campaign with Facebook, Twitter, Google+, LinkedIn and email. It has live chat "coaching" assistance to help you start up.

Fees and Payments: Fundrazr permits you to choose between PayPal or Wepay to process your donations and payments. They charge 5%, plus credit card or payment provider fees of 2.9% and thirty cents a transaction. This is a total 7.9%+ per donation. Donors can pay using PayPal, credit card or bank debit. As per their Website, "All contributions are deposited instantly" into your PayPal or WePay account.

GOFUNDME, www.gofundme.com. "Crowdfunding for Everyone!" It calls itself the world's #1 fundraising site, and has the GoFundMe mobile app. There are no goal requirements and no penalty for missing your goal. Keep every donation you receive.

Fees and Payments: 5% plus 2.9% for payment processing through Wepay = 7.9% plus $0.30 per donation.

GOGETFUNDING, www.gogetfunding.com. "We're a personal crowdfunding Website where you can raise money for anything that matters to you. From personal causes and projects to events & more." Partial funding allowed. It can receive money over your fundraising goal if your campaign reaches its goal before the time expires. Also the site allows ongoing fundraisers. Funding allowed in most major currencies, however, requires a PayPal or Stripe account to receive the money you raise.

Fees and Payments: Charges 4%, which is automatically deducted when you receive a donation. Also must pay PayPal and Stripe charges.

INDIEGOGO, www.indiegogo.com. "The World's Crowdfunding Engine." Site states it supports 5 currencies and 4 languages. You can select either a flexible fund-raising campaign where you get paid even if you do not reach your goal, or a fixed fundraising campaign where your contributors get refunds if you do not reach your goal. It states it supports more fundraising categories than any other platform. Site has a writing category. Fund seekers include authors seeking money for their book tours, and even publishers funding their "pre-sale launch party."

Fees and Payments: Has multiple fund raising models. Charges 5% plus 3% and $.30 per donation for credit-card transactions or 3-5% for PayPal transactions. No fees for fixed funding campaigns that do not reach their goal.

KAPIPAL, www.kapipal.com. All types of crowd funding. Maximum length of a campaign is one year. You can continue to receive donations after the goal amount is reached. Full funding is not required, and according to their Website, "you can start your Kapipal again to try to collect more money.

Fees and Payments: Charges 4% with PayPal's credit card processing fees (In the US, that's 2.9%, plus $0.30 a donation) additional.

KICKSTARTER, www.kickstarter.com.

Fees and Payments. Kickstarter charges a 5% fee for funds collected, and their payment processor charges another 3-5%.

Crowd funding has been used successfully to publish many books, including all genres of novels, picture books, educational and how-to books. However, with rising awareness, crowd funding sites are getting....well....crowded. Well.... Crowded.

Fire Starter # 58-Stand out among the crowd

To stand out among the many authors asking for funds, develop a pitch using at least one of these fire starting ideas:
1. Explain why the book is special (and important to you), and how much you want others to enjoy it. Be authentic. Convey your passion for writing and how difficult it is to build awareness for your book in today's market. Tug on their emotions and you have a better chance of getting funded;
2. Humanize your pitch with a two-minute video. Use humor if it fits. Otherwise, tell a compelling story that creates an emotional connection. Make a personal appeal on the video, even if you're camera shy. Supporters want to know who they are donating money to. Don't forget to mention other creative projects, books, etc. that will help build trust in you;
3. Include any pictures, drawings, illustrations, etc. to showcase the cover, characters, or places in the book. Pictures help draw the contributor into your story;

4. Include an excerpt or writing sample; include an excerpt on your blog page and link to that page from the crowd funding, proposal site;

5. Remember to integrate your crowd funding campaign with your other social media sites. Cross link and make sure you direct people to the crowd funding site from your social media sites;

6. If you are planning a series, include a brief synopsis of the rest of the books in the series. Make sure you show people where you are headed and how big your dreams are;

7. Identify your target audience, and tell donors who will like the book...."This book will be enjoyed by—";

8. Tell them exactly how the money will be spent. For book publishing, you may be inclined to include the following cost categories: book-cover design, illustrator, editor, print, marketing, etc. To generate even more interest, develop a creative marketing campaign (Antic Ad concept, video series, event, game, an interactive tool);

9. Create a unique tee shirt with the cover design, title, or excerpt from the book and offer as a reward for contributing. Show a picture of the tee shirt on the proposal page;

10. Offer to name a character after the donor; this offer should be reserved for the highest donor level and make sure to limit the number who can receive this reward.

This Worked For: Kris White, author of the graphic novel, *The 36.* Kris offered to name a character after contributors who were willing to shell out $1,000.00 each. According to his Kickstarter page, contributors at this level could have "your likeness immortalized as a supporting character in the book." He limited this opportunity to four donors. Kelly Thompson and her young adult book, *The Girl Who Would Be King.* After being rejected by New York's finest publishers, Kelly decided to take her book to the public via Kickstarter. She exceeded her budget by 330% and earned more in crowd funding before her book was published than most traditionally published authors ever do! It also worked for Brant Cooper and Patrick Blaskovics'' *The Lean Entrepreneur,* which had close to $12,000.00 in pre-sales at InvestedIn.

Additional Resources: To learn more about crowd funding, check out Scott Steinberg's **FREE** downloadable book, *The Crowd funding Bible* at *http://*www.crowd fundingguides.com.

Make A Blaze In Your Own Backyard:
Develop an effective Grass-Roots Campaign to elevate your book to "local hero" status.

First, go local. Take advantage of YOUR town and YOUR local writing community for support. These are your best resources to get started. Not only will you find unexpected resources; you'll find a group of people who understand you like no one else.

Fire Starter # 59-Get involved in your community college.

Go online to local colleges or universities that have writing programs and find out when they're having readings. This type of event attracts all kinds of writers like moths to a flame. That's where you're likely to find a supportive group of people to help you navigate your book launch.

Fire Starter # 60-Become a major donor

Donate signed books and/or gift baskets featuring your book with items supporting its theme, characters, or setting to non-profits. Charities and schools frequently have at least one seasonal fundraiser, like a silent auction or raffle. Make sure and include a bio card from your press kit with contact information and your Web site so people know where to follow up for additional information. Encourage the event host to set a low opening bid for your donation to encourage bidding. Everyone who sees your book, including winners and losers, are all potential future buyers of your book. Finally, check and see if your event host is giving out gift bags with sponsor items to the attendees, and if so, make sure and include a magnet or bookmark referencing your book and Web site. This basically guarantees attendees will look at your name and book at least twice!

Fire Starter # 61-Find captured audiences in your area.

Captured Audiences are people who attend an event and for reasons of family connection, social involvement, political networking, business networking or other social reasons, are committed to staying for the event's entirety. Many times they've arrived early to obtain good seats or a strategic location and had time before the event begins when their attention is freed up to focus on other things. Local organizations offer many opportunities for you to connect with the Captured Audience.

$-$$ Low to Moderate Cost

High school sports teams, clubs, and theater, and community theaters offer events with Captured Audiences. The sports teams often hang signs from sponsors around their venue for the entire season. You don't have to have a child participating in the program or even attending the school to leverage this advertising opportunity. Theaters typically have programs printed by the season or show, with rates below a hundred dollars. Again, an actual connection to the school or theater is not usually required. Both choices guarantee that your name, Web site and book title will be read by hundreds if not thousands of people. Note-you will have two costs involved: the cost of your ad design, or sign production if it's for a sports team, and the sponsorship cost.

$$-$$$ Moderate to Major Bucks

Don't discount the pre-movie slide show at local theaters. You might be surprised at how cheaply you can procure a slot. Be sure to ask if you can focus your ad campaign so that your slide is shown at movies drawing an audience that includes your target demographic.

Fire Starter # 62-Light fires at fairs and festivals

You're missing opportunities if you limit your festival search to book fairs and those featuring authors. Sometimes it's better to be one of only a few authors at the party! Contact local authorities to see if you can set up an "author's table" at community events such as craft shows, farmer's markets, state fairs, etc. If they insist on charging you a premium, see whether your local library or arts group will sponsor the table. If this is "no go," get together with some author friends who write in the same or compatible genres and split the table cost. Make sure when you attend you have multiple copies of your book displayed and ready to sell and lots of book marks, magnets and other giveaways.

Fire Starter # 63-Become a book-reading, group-guru

Solicit local book reading groups. Book reading groups love to have author visits, and many will read books from local authors. Put together a special postcard campaign targeting these groups in your area. Offer a "book club package" with a discount off the cover price for volume purchases, swag bags with bookmarks, magnets and other glitz to sweeten the deal, and for the larger clubs, offer to come and speak to the groups in person for free after their group has read your book. Where to find these groups? Look on Facebook and Google+. You can also twitter about it, set up a special page on your Web site just for book clubs, and get the word out through your local library and arts groups.

Fire Starter # 64-Connect & partner with your local gate keepers

Gatekeepers are those individuals who have special standing to prohibit or allow access to a particular group. It is definitely worth cultivating the gatekeepers in your area for those groups that closely match your ideal reader demographic.

Create a partnership based on setting: Every genre has a fan club with a local fan base and local gate keepers to that fan base. If you write wine country, murder mysteries, your local fan group includes a subset of wine country lovers. Establish a relationship with a nearby vineyard, include it as a setting in your book, then see whether they will carry your book on a commission basis in their gift shop, on their Web site and as part of their seasonal gift baskets.

Do you write books featuring a Goth teenage, ghost detective? Find out where your local Goth teenagers hang out- include a store or street from that area in your book and network with local merchants to create space for your book in their stores. Look at your book very carefully to see if the setting is one way to tie into groups of potential readers and then find the gatekeepers to those groups.

Create a partnership based on a win-win relationship. Are you writing for small or middle-grade children? Then establish relationships with their gatekeepers by providing a tie-in to your book that helps the gatekeepers relate your book to the children in their custody.

For teachers, provide lesson plans, for Girl Scout and Boy Scout leaders, provide badge activities, for Sunday school teachers provide bible quotes and lessons, and for camp, counselors provide games and songs...yes, songs. Find a local musician and write a jingle for your book. This could prove to be a great promotional tool!

Create a partnership based on the writers' journey. Even if your book is so general in nature it seemingly applies to everybody, or micro- with a limited audience, remember you have something to leverage in addition to the book that many folks are interested in learning more about - your writer's journey. You can develop lesson plans, games, bible quotes, and badge activities all based on your personal journey as a writer.

Need more ideas to get your local audience fired up? Read on below:

1. Send press releases to your local media at least two weeks before the big day.
2. Host a book b-day party at your local library with giveaways and promos.
3. Donate a book to your public library, and, if appropriate, to all the school libraries in your area.
4. See if the local Welcome Center or Chamber of Commerce will accept a donation of your book to keep on hand in the visitor's center.

5. Offer to talk to local chapters of certain national non-profit organizations such as Kiwanis, Rotary Club, Toastmasters, or the Women's Business Association about a topic related to your book, or about your experiences as a writer.

6. If your community has a local news cable station, call the producer to see if you can either be interviewed for a news show, or run a mock newscast you script and film for their use.

7. Ask your local consignment stores to carry a few copies of your book on consignment. Be sure to get them to sign for a set number of copies and negotiate shelf space with good traffic flow.

8. Approach local businesses like restaurants, especially the ones with retail space attached, and ask whether they will carry your book.

9. Look for retail outlets that specialize in locally made products and ask them to carry your book.

Additional Resources:

Learn more at: What Is a Grassroots Marketing Strategy? | eHow.com http://www.ehow.com/info_7942836_grassroots-marketing-strategy.html#ixzz28Hx9hxdp

This Worked For: Meg Medina, author of the award winning "Yaqui Delgado Wants to Kick Your Ass." Meg takes her involvement with her community very seriously, co-sponsoring with her hometown library a yearly festival that honors other writers. She urges writers to get involved in their communities and become good "Literary Citizens."

PART THREE: KEEP THE FIRES BUILDING DURING PUB MONTH AND BEYOND

It's one thing to connect to your readers, it's quite another to maintain that relationship and nurture it until it grows into a long term fan base. This section focuses on those things you need to do to enable readers to find you and allow you to retain them.

Use Google to Light a Flame Under Your Book Sales:

$ to Free!

GOOGLE BOOKS, PARTNER PROGRAM & GOOGLE PLAY: DEAD OR ALIVE?

Well, it is unclear if Google play, Books Partner Program has been consigned to the Google graveyard. Apparently, as of spring 2015, here is the notice that was/is posted at the entry page for the sign-up form:

> We are not accepting new sign-ups at this time. We are sorry for the inconvenience. We'll be back soon.

We are including the information below in case Google back-tracks on this decision.

In 2010, Google introduced Google Books. With the Google Books Partner Program, you can promote your books on Google for **FREE.** If you are self pubbed, here's where you begin: https://accounts.google.com/NewAccount?service=printpublisher&hl=en_US&ltmpl=books&continue=https://books.google.com/partner/signon&gsessionid=eGOdrMJyCHJM4_eYmlBk2A.

*NOTE! You have to sign into your Google account before you can access this page. If you do not have a Google account, then the link will take you to a form where you can set up one.

If you have a publisher, you may need them to enroll you in the program. By submitting your book for inclusion in Google's search results, you can increase awareness of your book at no cost and direct interested people to your Web site. Here is how it works; Google Books scans your book and matches the content in your book with user searches. That means, the people who see your book are qualified leads; they are the people most interested in buying your book. You can also embed a provided code into your Web site, which allows potential buyers to preview your book on your Web site.

NOTE: As of October 2015, the Google Play Bookstore is still selling books!

Google now also sells eBooks directly at Google Play: https://play.google.com/store/books. Formatted for smart phones and tablets, books purchased through Google Play are not compatible with Kindle. To sell books through Google Play, you must first set up your book for the preview program. Here's where to find the nitty-gritty on selling books through Google Play: http://support.google.com/books/partner/bin/static.py?hl=en&topic=1346917&guide=1346912&page=guide.cs&answer=1619765.

However, the link below to set up a selling account takes you back to the notice above that they are not accepting new partners at this time. https://support.google.com/books/partner/checklist/4489282

It is unclear whether existing partners can add new books and/or for how long the Google Play Bookstore will continue operating.

Well, we did tell you so! Here's some prescient words from our first edition of 100 Small Fires:

A few words of caution: Google does not post its sales revenue split for books sold through Play. Apparently, it reserves the right to negotiate different terms of sale with different publishers. Also, Google is notorious for changing its policies and terms of services.

They even have their own warnings in this regard posted on their information page for Google Play as follows:

Publisher Program Policies for Books on Google Play in the U.S.

Please note that we may change our policies at any time, and it is your responsibility to keep up-to-date with and adhere to the policies posted here. We will notify account holders via email upon changes to these policies.

OTHER WAYS TO USE GOOGLE TO ADD FIRE TO YOUR BOOK SALES:

GOOGLE ALERTS

If you have a Gmail account you can set-up Google Alerts. *https://www.google.com/alerts*

Google will email you an "alert" every time, there is new content posted on the Web that is triggered by your alert search terms. You can set your alerts to digest form for period compiling to keep these incoming emails from clogging up your inbox.

The usefulness of this tool is only limited by your creativity. You can use alerts for find bloggers actively posting books similar to yours that may be open to hosting a leg of your book tour. You can use alerts to keep you abreast of book-related events and happenings in your hometown that might provide avenues for book sales. You can use alerts to notify you of book contests or agents or publishers open to queries. You can research other books in your writing genre. You can use alerts to track your own books and yourself! You can use alerts to research topics of interest for your writing.

Fires Starter # 65-Set up a Google Wallet.

$-Free to Low Cost

In our last edition, we took you through the steps to set up a Google Check-out. That product has been consigned to the Google Graveyard, and they have replaced it with Google Wallet. Google

Wallet is designed to complete with PayPal, Amazon Payments, Apple Pay and other on-line payment services.

Here is the link to the intro page to Google Wallet. https://www.google.com/wallet/ .

One notable advantage provided by Google Wallet is that it is integrated into Gmail and allows users to send money through Gmail attachments. If you have built up a database of potential purchasers, particularly if you have a series, or strong sales from your Website, this is a valuable tool for direct marketing campaigns.

Fire Starter # 66-Use Google+ Hangout to fire up book clubs

If you haven't checked out Google+ lately there is one feature that is sure to win you over - Google+ Hangout. This is a great way to interact with a book club, an online writing group or a small group of readers. You can sell book club packages from your Web site, and include an hour of noshing with the author. The site offers **FREE** video chatting for up to ten people. Unfortunately, this means your online book club maximum number has to be nine (you'll use the tenth slot), if they are located in separate locations. A simple go around is to have more than one club member share an account log-in and trade off camera time. However, you should make this clear in your marketing materials so the book club knows exactly what they are getting.

You can also offer a similar deal for other groups, or even random fans willing to share the experience.

Limitations? Well, there's that maximum ten user thing. Additionally, everyone participating on a different monitor has to have a Google+ account for logon purposes.

For more information on Google+ Hangouts, see: http://www.google.com/+/learnmore/hangouts/

*HOT TIP. Skype video chatting is a good alternative for arranging visits between an author and a larger group of people who are in one location.

This Worked For: Kevin Kelly, an editor for *Wired* magazine, used a variation of this to promote his book, *What Technology Wants.*

Fire Starter # 67-Use Hangout to broadcast your presentation

Need to reach a large audience and develop some permanent content for your Web site? Google+ Hangout also allows you to broadcast your program to the world with a few easy steps. Just check "Enable Hangouts on Air" when you start a hangout, and Google+ posts your live hangout publicly on your profile, your You Tube channel and your Web site. Afterwards, the recording is sent to your You Tube channel and to your original Google+ post.

This can also be used for author readings. In the months prior to your book's birthday, broadcast yourself reading several chapters of your book to a small, but rapt audience. Giving away a free taste is a great way to get people to buy the whole loaf.

Light A Fire On Amazon:
Strategies to Achieve the Best Placement/Sales on Amazon

$-Free, Free, Free!

For those of you who don't get out much, Amazon is more than just a huge click-and-buy book store. It is a multi-faceted community of readers and writers, movie watchers and makers, bloggers and blog followers, musicians and music lovers, grocery stores and foodies, and fashionistas and boutiques. WARNING: Enter the world of Amazon at your own risk… it can be a HUGE time suck.

That's the downside. On the upside, the site contains tons of the latest information on how to fire up your sales in their bookstores, and they give it all away for **FREE.** Knowing how overwhelming it can be exploring all Amazon has to offer, we compiled some links and tips to help get you started. Consider those detailed below absolute **MUSTS.**

Fire Starter # 68–Leverage all of Amazon's FREE tools

Amazon has many **FREE** tools authors can use to help readers find their books and create greater visibility. These include customer reviews, tags, rankings, Listmania ® Lists, *So You'd Like to… Guides,* and *Search Inside the Book* ®. Here's the link where Amazon has a detailed list of these freebies together with links to other pages explaining in detail how each tool works: *How to Leverage Tools on Amazon.com to Increase Your Sales Opportunities.*

https://www.CreateSpace.com/en/community/docs/DOC-1009.

Note: "Likes" and "Tags" Have Been Phased Out! Amazon phased out the tagging tool. You can no longer use tags to direct potential readers to your book page. See here for more information:

https://www.amazon.com/gp/help/customer/display.html?ie=UTF8&nodeId=16238571&redirect=true

From investigation, it would appear that Amazon has also done away with the "Like" buttons you used to find at the top of every author's page and every book page. While, there doesn't seem to be a formal acknowledgment of this on the Website, a review of ten author pages, and approximately twenty book pages did not turn up a single "Like."

Fire Starter # 69-Claim your Author's Page

Claim your Author's Page on Amazon. Go to: http://www.authorcentral.com. On your page, be sure to fill out every data entry box, including adding pictures and images. Share some details about yourself, your likes and hobbies. Leave links back to your Web site and blogs. Don't make everything on your page a hard sell for your book. Ask readers to help you out by leaving reviews of your books. Do not assume your readers will know how to do this, or that they will be self-motivated to do this on their own. Remember, people are more likely to take action when there's a personal appeal.

HOT TIP! If you have your book for sale via Kindle Stores in other countries, make sure you setup an Author's Page at each country's store!

Fire Starter #70 - Brag About Events On Your Author's Page (and Elsewhere)!

Amazon lets you list your events, so use your author's page to list away! Log in to your Author's Page and scroll to the bottom. Beneath "Blogs," you will see "Events." Click on "add an event"" to the far right. This will bring up a form for adding events to your page. Now, while the form is tailored for venue-tied physical events, game it to add your cyber events, such as blog tours, and giveaways! There is no restriction on the "Description" section, so include links to your Website, your blog tour links, etc. You can also use the "Venue" line to add your Website address as well.

$-$$$ - Free to the Sky's the Limit! KDP Select Campaigns!

If you are a Kindle Direct Publishing (KDP) Select member, you can run several types of campaigns, including "Kindle Countdown Deal," "Kindle Free Book Promotion" (Free Days) and even purchase ads to sell your book. Simply login to your KDP account, and select the book you wish to advertise. Click on "Promote and advertise," and follow the directions to start your campaign. To the left of your book shelf, you'll see the buttons for Kindle Countdown Deal and Free Days. Read more about these important marketing tools below. To the right, you'll see the button to create an ad campaign. This is a new feature Amazon rolled out in 2015.

You can start an ad campaign for as little as $100.00. You pay per click through at rates averaging between $.20 per click and $.45 per click depending on the categories you where you choose to advertise. The more you agree to pay per click, the more clicks you will receive. You select the time frame over which your campaign

will run. From review of author comments in the Amazon KDP community blog, it appears that authors with book series seem to be fairly satisfied with the results of their ad campaigns. Here's the link to that thread at Amazon:
https://kdp.amazon.com/community/thread.jspa?threadID=222782

HOT TIP! It takes Amazon between 24 hours and three business days to approve an ad campaign, so plan ahead!

READ BELOW IF YOU ARE PRINTING YOUR BOOK!

Create Space, the paper book publishing arm of Amazon, provides some **FREE** tools to help you self-publish and distribute your books. If you're planning on printing with Create Space, check out the Fire Starters below:

Fire Starter # 71-Join Amazon Advantage BEFORE you publish!*

Joining Amazon Advantage provides expanded distribution of your paper book. Joining it allows you to do several things you cannot otherwise do. These include having a pre-order button for your book. You can list your book on Amazon as soon as you have an ISBN number. Using Advantage, you can also do pre-publishing day sales. This is important when you don't have control over your book pub date, or if you are planning big events around your pub date. There are merchandising and advertising opportunities you can take advantage of as an Advantage Member who are not open to non-members. Joining Amazon Advantage is also rumored to speed up the time between approval through Create Space and availability for sale at Amazon. At $29.00 a year, this one's a no brainer. Here's where you can read more about Amazon Advantage:

https://www.amazon.com/gp/seller-account/mm-product-page.html?topic=200329780

*NOTE, other voices to the contra; Here is an excellent article on why you should NOT join Amazon Advantage written by a blogger named "Skywriter."

.

Skywriter recommends using Create Space to distribute on Amazon, and Ingram Spark/Lightning Source to distribute to local bookstores and libraries worldwide. Here's the address for that publisher: https://www.ingramspark.com/ and you can read more on Lightning Source below.

However, make sure to submit your book for printing in time to meet your deadline. Note that times may vary widely. Without Amazon Advantage, it can take Create Space 4-6 weeks after approval to have your book ready and for it to appear in the Amazon bookstore. Factor at least six weeks into your schedule if you plan on it showing up before a certain season or holiday. In a time crunch? Consider using another print-on-demand company. Lightning Source (see below) has speedier print times and may be a better option to get your book out before your deadline.

Fire Starter # 72-Pre-order your own book to speed up Buy-it-Now time

Put in a pre-order with Create Space or other book printer/distributers, so your book shows up as available for purchase on your publication date. By placing a pre-order for a set number of books, your book will have a buy-it-now button on your pub date instead of an "available for a pre-order"" notice.

Fire Starter # 73-Make sure you buy your own ISBN #

$-$$ Low to Moderate

Make sure to secure your own ISBN # from www.bowker.com so that if you decide to use other print/distribution services in the future, you will be able to keep the same ISBN number. While the discounted or free ISBN #'s are tempting to use, they do lock you into Create Space (or Lulu if you use theirs). A different ISBN is needed for every published version of a book. You will need a separate one if you start with Create Space and Amazon's Expanded Distribution Channels and then decide to switch. ISBN#'s cost approximately $125.00 for a single number and $250.00 for ten.

*Note: If you don't use Create Space for your design, printing and distribution, you can still get your POD or printed books distributed overseas. You will need to go to Amazon for each targeted country and follow their listing procedures. Another option is to use a different design and print-on-demand company that has those distribution channels. Lulu, at www.lulu.com is one such company. A third option requires that you have a print-ready book. Lightning Source is a printer/distributor used by publishers. Due to their relationship with Ingram Book Company – the world's largest wholesale book distributor – Lightning Source can distribute your book just about anywhere. They offer print on demand services with a wide distribution network, quality product, and speedy print times. They do require that your book comes pre-typeset to their specifications. See www.lightningsource.com.

HOT TIP*: Some authors use Create Space for design and US orders and then Lightning Source for distribution of international orders.

Create Space has tips on how to leverage the tools in Amazon to increase book sales. See;
https://www.CreateSpace.com/en/community/docs/DOC-1009

Amazon is the number-one market for eBooks, and has Create Space; it's very competitive, print-on-demand arm. Hence, it's worth the time required to make sure you are proactive in kindling your flames there.

This weekend, spend several hours doing just that. Try to use at least a few of the tools they provide to become familiar with how they work. Then calendar yourself to spend a couple of a week deepening your connection with their tools. Write lists, write guides, write reviews. All these tools give readers opportunities to get to know you and buy your books.

Keep Your Fires Blazing Using Email and Twitter:

Transform Readers to Fans

Earlier in this book, we made the case for email and discussed strategies to start building your email marketing list. Now, let's review a few strategies for using this list to generate book sales and long-term relationships.

One Fire Starter #74-Consumer focused content always wins.

One great way to develop long-term relationships with your target audience is to create unique and exclusive content that can be delivered via email to people who opt-in to receive your newsletter, tip sheets, white papers etc. Earlier we talked about how to create content for content marketing.

It's important, however, to distinguish between consumer focused content relevant to your audience versus content that **you** would like to get/read. In previous chapters, we talked about the importance of identifying your target audience; the people most likely to enjoy/buy your book.

When you are marketing your book, that target audience should be at the center of everything you do. It helps sometimes to imagine an actual person. Let's say you are a romance fiction writer. You believe your target audience is typically a married female aged 30 to 50 years old. Now, craft a "persona" around that target. Give her a name and add some details of her life. Create her "story." Cindy is 49, married with two children in their late teens. She is working outside the home and extremely busy. Her husband owns his a business and travels constantly. They are two ships passing in the night. And so on and so on. Perhaps she has financial trouble. Perhaps she dotes on her pets because she is lonely. Keep this up until you have a clear picture of this person. Now, with Cindy in mind (as well as your major book themes or big ideas) develop content for your email marketing campaign that you believe Cindy would like to read. If you are unsure, see what types of research you can find on the Internet regarding your target audience. For example, you may be able to find out which Web sites are frequented by your target segment, which should give you an idea of their interests.

Check out these sites to get you started:

www.alexa.com, Web site statistics-search by category

https://support.google.com/adwords/answer/3278806, explains, "Display Planner," an AdWords tool "that helps you build your direct response or brand campaigns for the Display Network."

www.pewinternet.org, Pew Research Centers who provides numbers, facts and trends.

One sure-fire method of identifying relevant content is to ask your target audience; what types of content would you like to see in your newsletter? You could create a quick and dirty poll or survey or ask your network, contacts or Facebook friends directly. In addition, don't forget your competition. What types of content are other romance writers or mystery writers or thriller writers, including on their blogs, Web sites, in their emails or newsletters? Find an author who is in your genre but has been doing this for a while and study their blogs or Web sites for ideas.

Fire Starter # 75-Go viral with a Victorian introduction

It's time to launch your book and therefore, you turn to your email list and start crafting the message that will go to everyone on your list. Some of the people on your list know you very well and will read your email as soon as they get it. Others won't know you as well and may be apt to ignore your message. Additionally, you want your book launch message to reach as many people as possible, but you want to avoid spamming people you don't know. That's not a good way to start a relationship. So how to make your email seem important enough for someone you don't know very well to read it? This is a vexing challenge, and we have a solution.

Anyone familiar with the works of Jane Austen knows that in Victorian times, a lady had to be formally introduced to a stranger before she could talk to them. The introduction was part of a vetting process to ensure the stranger was of a sufficient caliber to merit an instance of familiarity. These days with the floods of spam we all experience, we need a similar vetting process to ensure our email is read, and our solicitation considered. So instead of asking your friends and family to buy your book, ask them to be a "book launch day party sponsor." All they do is forward your email invite to your online book launching event to a select group of their friends they think may be interested.

Be sure and spice up your invite with a chapter or first page of your book to hook the readers. Also, add some special offers. For example, have your invite include a special incentive for responders who buy your book on the book launch day, such as free swag if they reply to the invite with a copy of their sales receipt and home address. Or, offer to video chat with any book club buying your book on launch day that has ten members or more.

Finally, get your invite to go viral by asking each reader to become a sponsor too. Make sure and give special swag or even a free book to anyone who sends your invite to 15 (you pick the number) or more friends or relatives.

Use this same "sponsorship" idea to promote sales, specials, book club packages, birthday party packages; be creative but don't wear out your email contacts. Limit your requests to one every couple of months and be sure to thank and reward everyone who responds. Use this technique and you'll be well on your way to building that golden list of 5,000+ sure fire buyers.

Fire Starter # 76-Seed your email with social media "share" links for viral fire starters

Adding social media "share" links to your emails will improve the chances of your email going viral. These links let the recipient share your book announcement with their Facebook friends or Twitterverse, or Google+ Circle. Social media shares give you the best chance for your content to go viral; as a reminder, going viral means your message will spread like wildfire at high speed across the universe at little or no cost to you. Sound good? Of course, it does. That's why we have given you a variety of tips to help your content go viral. When an email subscriber shares your message with their social network, it can reach their entire network, and then their friends and families network and so on.

So, to increase the chance that your message will go viral, not only do you want to add "share" links, but also think of the type of content you are sending. Is it the type of content that is likely to be shared? Can you build in a viral component by adding incentives so subscribers will want to share?

Fire Starter # 77-Use squeeze pages to improve response

$-$$ Free to Moderate Cost

A squeeze page is a single web page with the sole purpose of capturing email addresses for follow-up marketing. A true squeeze page means there are no exit hyperlinks from the page. Your only choice is to give up your email address or leave the site altogether.

A good squeeze page is short, to the point, with a clear and compelling call to action. Sweeten the pot (and take the sting out of the "squeeze") by offering a sign up bonus: "Sign up now and receive a free bookmark!"

Aggressive strategies - like presenting visitors with multiple incentives in exchange for their contact information - are frequently used with good success. The ultimate goal of the squeeze page is to get the email address for follow up. Navigation or other links are typically absent from true squeeze pages. However, you have to decide how aggressive you want to get. If you don't want to box your visitor in, then a squeeze page can include one click-away link. The key is to get them to focus on your offer. If an offer to join your newsletter is presented on a crowded page, the visitor may get distracted and click away from the page before you get the email address.

Squeeze pages are easy to set up. Just search "free squeeze page template for WordPress" or an appropriate variation thereof, and you'll find a bunch of options. They can be used in conjunction with email drip campaigns (see below) and auto-responders, which send an automatic "welcome" message to the subscriber as soon as they subscribe to your list. For a few bucks, you can get more comprehensive templates with customer assistance from a variety of vendors. Change your search from free to "low cost," to find a hundred choices.

This Worked For: Dave Ramsey uses a squeeze page on his Web site promoting his book *EntreLeadership.* Go to http://www.entreleadership.com/home/ and follow the links to "bonus online resources." In order to gain access to bonus materials and resources, you have to give Dave your email address in a squeeze page.

Fire Starter # 78–Use email drip campaigns to your advantage

$ - $$$ Free to Major Bucks

As we have stated before, turning a mildly interested prospect into a buying customer often takes multiple "touch points" or contacts. For smaller email lists, you can blind copy your recipients on Yahoo or Gmail, and administer your campaign yourself. Be sure to maintain a database of your comma separated emails in a word processing file independent of your email account. This will give you more flexibility in using other message delivery systems in the future should you choose.

Nurturing relationships over time can be a daunting task, especially when your email list gets longer than 500+ contacts, and you are trying to send out at least a monthly newsletter. This is where email drip marketing campaigns come into play. They can be an efficient and cost effective tool for staying in touch with your prospects.

An email drip campaign sends a series of emails that you write in advance to prospects over time at regularly scheduled intervals. By sending repeated messages automatically, you can stay connected with your prospects until they are ready to buy. The drip campaign is typically triggered after the prospect signs up for your newsletter online.

If you are just starting out and launching your first book, you may want to create and execute the drip campaign on your own or manually. If you are on your second or third book, have a significant mailing list (in the hundreds or thousands) and need help managing your leads, it may be time to consider buying software or a system like www.ConstantContact.com or www.AllClients.com to develop and execute an email marketing drip campaign. According to AllClients, "even the most novice user can use drip marketing by creating drip email marketing campaigns in AllClients." Other bulk emails sending services are www.mailchimp.com and www.hubspot.com. . Mailchimp will allow you to email up to 2000 people 6 times a month for free. Other plans begin at $25.00 per month and go up from there depending on the number of subscribers you have and how often you contact them.

You could set up your drip campaign to deliver an email once a month until your book launch date. Or, for the more technologically advanced marketer, you could set up a more complex campaign that segments your prospects into different categories. For example, you could have a separate drip campaign for previous customers versus new customers. Regardless of your campaign goals-build relationships, sell books or build credibility as an expert - offer value with each email. This may include links to articles or blogs relevant to your book topic or special offers and promotions.

In the business of book promotion, building relationships with your readers/fans is very important. For a drip campaign to current customers, think of ways you can offer value without promotional messages. Send greeting cards, birthday well wishes and interesting content. Request feedback - everyone likes to be asked their opinion so encourage them to hit the "reply" button or to take a survey.

Fire Starter # 79–Gamify your email campaign

Adding game elements to your email campaign is a great way to engage your prospects. We cover Gamification in more depth later in this section.

Email Marketing Worked For: Not surprisingly, more than one best-selling author swears that the email list is "The Thing." John Locke, author of the Donovan Creed Series, states that his goal is to have an email list of ten thousand guaranteed buyers of his books. With over 25 books for sale on Amazon as of October 2015, ten thousand guaranteed buyers would equal 260,000 units sold. With eBooks priced at to $2.99 and his paperbacks at $9.99 a book, moving that number of books equals a serious cash flow. To develop and maintain his list of buyers, John Locke spends a lot of time on Twitter, interacting with people who fall within his target audience or can relate to the themes in his books. He also tries to respond to all readers' emails and works hard to maintain his list, spending several hours a day interacting with those folks already on it.

Keep Your Fires Blazing At Your Home Base: Two weeks before Launch Day:

Write one month of blog postings, two weeks of postings for before your designated book launch day, and postings for two weeks after. Build excitement with the posts, including contests and giveaways. This way, on *The Day*, you'll be ready to go and only have to make a few updates or upload pictures and media. Make sure and offer giveaways such as mugs, bookmarks, signed copies of your book, etc. to the first ten readers to post feedback on Goodreads, Shelfari and/or Amazon. Send out emails to alert your list of potential buyers, and Twitter about everything (with emphasis on the giveaways and not on the sales). You want your books to hit the shelves, stands and lists with fanfare and for sales to flame right away.

LAUNCH DAY!

You've lit your fires and have your book ready to go. Now, what to do on the actual day it hits the shelves or is listed in the Kindle categories?

Launch Party in the "Real" World, Yes or No?

Ok, let's be pragmatic about this. You can dump a lot of money into a physical launch party that may not result in increased book sales. If you are tied in with a local indie book store and can arrange to have one there that is the best way to go. If not, the expense and headache of renting a space, catering - even if it's only coffee, punch and cookies- and getting the word out (all to sell a dozen books) may or may not be worth it to you. If you've got to "see your baby off properly," open your wallet and launch away. Here's a great blog post with tips on how to do this right:

http://blog.bookbaby.com/2012/03/how-to-throw-a-book-launch-party-that-isnt-a-waste-of-time/.

Be sure and read the comments section for additional tips from other authors who have vetted the book launch party for you.

If all this sounds like way more hassle and cost than its worth, and most of your readers will be purchasing off of Amazon or IBookstore anyway, then do the next-best thing.

Fire Starter # 80-Make a big deal out of your small party

On your book launch day, reward visitors to your Web site with giveaways and promos. Let everyone who buys a book on this day register on your Web site for a fabulous prize and swag. Twitter about each prize drawing, announcing both the giveaway and the winner. Celebrate every milestone. You can keep your "party" simple and inexpensive (cupcakes work great for this), but still do something special to mark each time your flames leap a little higher.

Fire Starter # 81 - Fire up your fan base with pictures

Hollywood knows how to make an old street in the middle of Georgia look like the French Quarter in New Orleans-it's all in camera shots, lighting and picture angles. Steal some of their moxy by using pictures to make your event, no matter how fun and exciting, look even bigger and more thrilling! First, make sure you have the right props. If you have an eBook, print out your cover on heavy stock paper and tape to another book for depth and weight. Then, take plenty of pictures - pictures of your smiling face holding your book, pictures of you toasting a few friends as THEY hold copies of your book, and pictures of your book birthday cake or cupcake before the party. Pictures, pictures, pictures.

Here are some other pic op suggestions you can use for social media like Pinterest or to update content on your Web site and blog:
Your First-Hour pic op. Smile as you hold up a sign with a card bearing a number indicating total sales.
Your First 24 Hours/First Week/First Month Party
Your It's Five O'clock Some-where Party
Your Burn the Midnight Oil Party
Your first 500 sales party.
Your first 1000 sales party
Your first #____ sales party.

In our media-centric world, if there's a picture, there was an event, so be sure to take plenty of photographs for each "event," even if it's only a shot of that cupcake with a candle and your gleaming face behind it. Post pics to as many social media outlets as you can-Pinterest, your blog, Facebook and your Web site are minimums, and make sure you tag, tag, tag.

Fire Starter # 82-Focus your pics on your readers

Get your readers involved in the pic ops! Hold a "most excited" face contest and have your reader's send in *selfies or pictures of them holding your book. Have readers take pictures of themselves dressed like your characters and let other readers vote for the best. *Note-according to the Urban Dictionary, a selfie is a "a picture taken of yourself that is planned to be uploaded to Facebook, MySpace or any other sort of social networking Web site. You can usually see the person's arm holding out the camera...."

Let your readers share, your excitement and they'll want to help you spread the fun. Here are some ideas to get readers/fans engaged:

1. Develop a treasure hunt for items used in your book, and post clues on your blog. Set out the rules for the game on your blog before your book birthday, and then set a deadline for finding the clues for two weeks after your launch day. Award a prize to the reader who finds the most items.

2. Pick one distinct word from your book. Award a prize to the reader who guesses how many times that word is used in your book before your launch day. Get consumers involved/engaged with your book to motivate sales and create a loyal fan base. Get people involved in promoting your book while creating content that could help your book/story get picked up by the media. Think Mentos/Coke Geysor video contest as inspiration. That campaign went viral.

Fire Starter # 83-Keep your readers involved after Launch Day

1. Hold a contest for best acted out scene. Hire some amateur actors (film school) to act out one scene so you have a half way decent entry. Give a prize for best video and post to Web site.
2. Ask readers to create an alternate ending and give a prize for the best one.
3. Hold a contest for the best cover art/photo. Post these in a special area of your Web site, pin them on Pinterest, or even e-publish a special edition with the new cover and alternative ending.
4. Hold a contest for the best puppet skit of a scene, real or imagined, from your book (a.k.a. Harry Potter puppet skit on You Tube) and create a You Tube Channel just for these skits. Award a prize to the one that gets the most views.

Fire-Up Your Readers With A Blog Tour

A blog tour is typically a group of blogs you link to in a pre-determined order from your Web site or blog. On chosen date and at a designated time, the blogs will post reviews of your book, interviews of you and/or host a chat or twitter talk. The tour can last anywhere from a few days to a few months. Setting up a blog tour can cost as little as $100.00 to as much as several thousand dollars depending on whether you hire out the leg work or do it yourself, and on the costs of the giveaways, including books, swag and other freebies. These are usually awarded by each blog as a prize in a contest associated with your tour. One successful author actually gave away Kindles on his blog tour!

It's important to find, pitch to and promote in the right blogs to create the biggest fire possible with the least effort. Here's how to find the right bloggers for your tour:

$ As In FREE! Or Low Cost

Organize your own blog tour. Do this by consult directories and compiling your lists of bloggers who may be interested in reading and reviewing your book. Look for directories of bloggers who categorize blogs by book type, genre and age group. Here are a few:

http://bookbloggerdirectory.wordpress.com/;
http://bookblogging.net/
http://www.fsbmedia.com/book_blogger_search.php
http://bookbloggerlist.com/
http://bookblogs.ning.com

To find more, Google "book blog directories."

Another way to find appropriate blogs for your blog tour is to pick four or five books that are similar to yours. Find out, which blogs reviewed these books and have a decent amount of site traffic or blog followers.

Regardless of how many blog sites you select as targets for your tour, you will need to query each site owner at least six or more weeks in advance of your targeted tour date. Contact the blog owners to see if they'd like FREE advanced copies of your book in exchange for a review and/or interview. Send out advance copies at least three weeks (or when the blogger requires them) in advance of your launch day. Note, these do not necessarily have to be printed ARCs. Read the blogger's submission rules to make sure they accept emails or pdfs of the book. Most do these days. In addition, offer to send extra copies for giveaways and some book swag so the blogger owner can host a contest with prizes.

Make sure you list every leg of your tour on your own Web site with links and dates. See if you can get other author friends to do as well. Make sure you update your Facebook "Events" settings to reflect your tour dates and sites. See discussion of Linkies and Linky Tools below.

*HOT TIP! Make sure and ask whether the blogger will agree to allow your review to be re-posted after the blog tour on other sites, such as Goodreads, Amazon, and Shelfari.

Organize your tour with an app linking the blog tour sites. There are several free to low costs apps that can do this.

Free test links displaying your blog tour or circle members by name. Each tour member inserts a provided code into their blog page. No thumbnails or pictures supported. Good site. Easy to navigate.

Mister Linky's Magical Widget at www.blenza.com/linkies. This site has a "free text only" service for registered users which displays your blog tour members by name, and also offers a low subscription service with thumbnails or pictures instead of just names. It supports a variety of blogging platforms, including WordPress.com, WordPress (self-hosted), Blogger and LiveJournal. While it offers a variety of widgets for linking, some of them do cost a small fee, but even the paid subscriptions, here are inexpensive – the lowest being only $5.00 a year, and the highest $20.00.

InLinkz - www.InLinkz.com. Like Mister Linky's Magical Widget, this site offers free text linky lists, but you do have to pay for multiple thumbnails. Subscriptions run $1.99 per month, or $19.99 for twelve months.

Hire the pros to do it for you! $$-$$$ From Moderate to Major Bucks.

Does the research and email campaign required to set up a blog tour seem daunting? No worries. You can hire out the leg work and let someone else set up your blog tour for you. The pro of this is that you usually get at least 10 stops in your tour. The negative is that you have less control over your tour stops and sometimes a less targeted tour. You still have to provide each blogger/tour site with free books, book swag and other giveaways they can use to entice their readers. Find below some on the many blogs tours you can find on the Internet with a few minutes of searching.

http://www.goddessfish.com/tours.htm; It Specializes in all subgenres of romance fiction, YA and middle grade fiction, and other genre fiction like mysteries and science fiction. It requires two months advanced booking. Starts at $55.00 for a 10-12 "blurb" tour to $399.00 for a "full service, premium" book tour, including at least 30 tour stops over four weeks, and daily twitter promotion stated to be a $240.00 value. All tours must be booked between 4-8 weeks in advanced.

http://tlcbooktours.com/; Book eight weeks in advance for a 10 stop tour. It does not work with self-published authors. Must email for rates and information sheet.

http://xpressobooktours.com/services// Focusing on YA and New Adult and in business since 2012, xpressobooktours has some great disclosures regarding their social media presence. According to their Website, they have 1700 book tour hosts, 12,000 followers on Twitter, 5,700 followers on Goodreads, thousands of Facebook "likes" and has appeared in the Forbes' "Top 25 Goodreads Book Reviewers." They offer a $90.00 single day, book blitz, with an average of 60-80 signs ups, which can be booked on short notice;

however, they recommend 3-5 weeks. Their top of the line product is $280.00, and provides 40 tour stops.

http://bewitchingbooktours.blogspot.com/; Arranges paranormal, urban fantasy and paranormal erotica tours. Prices include $47.50 for a "Release Day Blitz" with postings on up to 20 blogs, $50.00 for a one-week tour with 5-7 stops and $200.00 for a month long "Virtual Tour Package" including coordination of radio interviews and a featured guest spot on Bewitching Radio.

http://yaboundbooktours.blogspot.com/p/services.html . Offers 15 stops for $50.00 to top product of 50 stops for $200.00. Tours must be booked 2-3 months in advance. Has testimonials on site.

HOT TIP* If it's in your budget, and you can find a blog tour company with access to a sufficient number of blogs having a clientele that mirror your target audience, hiring a blog tour company can save you oodles of time and can be worth every dollar. Make sure you research your blog tour company thoroughly before sending them any money. Look for testimonials on their site and follow along on a couple of their tours to see what they look like, and if they are the right fit for you and your book. Don't despair if you don't get around to booking your tour for several months after your book launch date. It took you considerable time to write your book, so be ready to take considerable time to market it.

Make Your Book Sales Roar With Audio!

$$ -Moderate to $$$- Major bucks

According to the Audio Publishers Association (APA), www.audiopub.org, audio book unit sales increased 19.5% between 2013 and 2014, with 25,787 titles published, an increase over 2013 by 1,032 titles. As per the organization's July 2015 press release:

"While adult titles continue to account for 87% of sales, children and young adult titles are on the rise with a 3.7% increase in sales from 2013 to 2014. The APA's recent consumer behavior study revealed a

113

strong demand for titles for younger listeners, with 36% of respondents reporting listening to children's or YA audio books. Fiction continues to represent the vast majority of audio books sold with roughly 77.4% of audios being fiction vs. 22.6% non-fiction. The unabridged format continues to dominate with 91% of audios sold being in this format." See:
http://www.audiopub.org/press/Sales_Survey_APA_2015_Final.pdf

Well, times have a changed since this book was first published in 2012. Flashback to those earlier days of audio books, and Amazon was so hungry for content for Audible (the Amazon arm used to sell audio books). They were willing to pay a premium. They sought to grow the number of available audio books by establishing "Audible Author Services" and a $20 million-dollar fund to back AAS through December 2012. This money was used to pay audio book authors $1 extra honorarium per sale for all sales through Audible.com, Audible.co.uk, and, yes, even iTunes.

Those days are over, but there is still good money to be made in audible books. After all, audio books are currently the largest growth area in publishing. These days, however, the author who uses a fee sharing producer has to split a 40% royalty with that producer (Amazon takes 60% of the sale as the retailer). The producer provides narration, recording and editing required for the final product. The alternative to this is to produce your own audio book or pay a production company a flat fee for this service. See below for more on those.

Finding a quality producer willing to work for a percentage of the royalty fee has recently been complicated by Amazon's sales strategy of offering a reduced-cost audio book bundled to an eBook sale. Coupled with Amazon's "Whispernet" technology, this offer is aimed at the reader who would like to switch between reading for him/herself and listening to the audio version. When an audio book is bundled with an eBook sale, the audio book is often priced as low as $1.99. This means that the author and producer have to share a royalty fee of 40% of $1.99 or $.80. Producers are unhappy with this reduction in profits they obtain from unit sales and as a result are more reluctant to take on projects under a fee splitting agreement.

Don't let this dissuade you from publishing an audio book! There are still quality producers who will work with you, but it may take a little longer to find one. And, there's always the other two options to enter this market: Produce your own or pay a producer out right for his/her or her or her services.

Fire Starter # 84-Produce it yourself.

Set up your home recording studio and produce and/or record it yourself.

Yes, due to advances in home recording studio equipment, it is possible to set up your own home recording studio and record your own audio book. You'll need a microphone, editing software, noise dampening headphones, possibly an audio interface, a computer, the willingness to tough out the learning curve and a VERY quiet space.

The approximate cost of setting up your own home recording studio (not including the cost of a quiet space, preferably a room with as close to absolute silence as you can manage) can vary wildly, running anywhere from several hundred dollars on the cheap side to several thousand. Amazon has an ACX wish list of studio equipment, here:

http://www.amazon.com/gp/registry/wishlist/2BKHP5PF3HNM0/ref =cm_sw_su_w. You can also download this list, and use it to shop elsewhere.

If you purchase everything listed, it will set you back about $675.00. This does not include the cost of your computer or other incidentals, such as quiet space, noise buffers, etc.

For more on setting up your own home studio see:

http://gizmodo.com/5900425/how-to-set-up-a-complete-home-recording-studio-for-under-2000

http://www.ehow.com/how_6865863_create-audiobook.html   and

http://www.acx.com/help/video-lessons-resources/200672590.

Discmakers.com offers a very helpful free booklet on setting up your own home studio. Find it here: http://www.discmakers.com/request/. They also offer several free marketing guides. Please note, however, the buying trend is away from books on discs to downloadable, digital books. The positive of this trend is that it is much cheaper to set up a studio for recording digital content. See below.

You can purchase a basic or pro package of the equipment you'll need from companies such as Sweetwater Music Instruments and Pro-Audio. Here are their addresses: http://www.sweetwater.com/store/wishlist.php?wlhash=0e191a5407afd3640a89c3342d1c0bdc
Sweetwater has a discount for ACX participants (see below); http://www.proaudio.com.

*HOT TIP! Unless you are using your studio to record content other than audio books, like music, you can save yourself some major bucks, and cut your learning curve in half, by going digital. With a digital microphone, you can forgo the audio interface needed for analog, i.e. non-digital, microphones.

These days it is possible to go fully digital and produce a product that meets industry standards for audio books. Rather than buy someone's pre-made package, you can save money by using a USB microphone and shopping around for the major components.

Besides the microphone (and various filters and stabilizers) you will need noise filtering headphones, an editing/compiling program, and a computer to run it all. For the microphone, try a Blue Yeti Pro USB Microphone on the higher end ($150.00 at the time of printing) or a Rode NT1A Anniversary Vocal Condenser Microphone Package ($229.00). Your microphone will need to record at levels exceeding the 16 bit/44.1 kHz standard used for recording audio CDs and be USB-ready. If you have a good quality, non-USB mike, consider the Blue Microphone Icicle XLR to USB converter.

For editing software, again, you can run the gamut between $ and $$$ bucks. On the low side is Audacity, which is a free source and often cited for its simplicity. Audacity can export in WAV, AIFF, AU, MP3 and OGG formats. You can download Audacity here:

http://audacity.sourceforge.net/.

$$$- Major Bucks

At this end of the spectrum are high-end programs like Pro Tools 10 ($600+) and the mid-rangers ($$) Sound Forge Pro 10 and Adobe Audacity, both of which will set you back approximately $300.00 or more.

$$- Moderate

Get your friends together and establish a studio co-op. While the cost of establishing a home studio with quality equipment may be prohibitive for any single author, it's the perfect project for a writers' group. Get your critique group of six or more together and you can drop that cost down to less than $200.00 a person. After that, you rotate the equipment through the group on an as-needed basis, and you will be selling audio books in no time!

Fire Starter # 85-Find the perfect narrator

$-As in Free or low cost to $$- Moderate Cost

If you've written a self-help, spiritual or how-to book or a fiction book where your voice matches that of your protagonist, and you have a good reading voice, you can narrate the book yourself. For help with this, check out online resources like https://www.acx.com/help/authors-as-narrators/200626860 and www.podiobooks.com. .

This Worked For: Neil Gaiman, who famously self-narrated *The Graveyard Book*; Malcolm Gladwell who narrated his books, *Outliers*, *The Tipping Point*, *Blink*, and *What the Dog Saw*; Scott

Sigler who narrated *Contagious*, *Infected*, and *Ancestor*; and Elizabeth Gilbert who narrates her best-selling self-empowerment books.

If you've got a frog croak for a voice and no frogs in your book, don't despair- there are many ways to find a suitable narrator. First, find out if any theaters, colleges or voice studios offer instruction in narrating audio books. If so, contact the program director and see if you can obtain the student roster or post to a student bulletin board. Students in these programs will often work for greatly reduced rates in order to establish a work history in this area. Second, contact your local high school drama and music departments for a YA teen voice, or college or university drama and/or music departments for an older, young adult voice. You may have to audition quite a few to find a suitable match for your character. If you need an older voice, contact some of the larger churches in your neighborhood and speak to the choir director for a referral. Another good source is your community theater.

$$- Major Bucks

If none of these efforts yield a suitable narrator, and you're blessed with a full purse, you can hire an expert. Find a professional narrator online. Here's a link to get you started: http://publishingcentral.com/audiobook/subject/audiobook-narrators/. You can also go on Audible, or other sites offering audio books, and listen to narrators. Audible actually has separate ratings for narrators which makes the site especially helpful for finding a narrator. Once you've found one you like, do a search for their Web site. If they are open to accepting new work, and not tied to any one studio or publisher, they normally will have a professional Web site with contact information. *Note: Many professional narrators will only work with established studios, while some have their own recording equipment. See below for Reelmusicianpro's quotes for studio production costs, including narration.

Hire it out to the Pros

If all of this sounds overwhelming, or you're time pressed, out-source the complete project.

$ - $$$ Nothing Up-Front to Major Bucks
Audio Book Creation Exchange, was developed by Audible, which is a subsidiary of Amazon. At http://www.acx.com it says:

> ACX is a marketplace where professional authors, agents, publishers, and other Rights Holders can post fallow audio book rights.
>
> At ACX, those unused audio rights will be matched with narrators, engineers, recording studios, and other producers capable of producing a finished audio book, as well as with audio book publishers.

The site has downloadable contracts and allows authors/publishers/agents to shop directly for professionals to produce their audio book. Amazon obtains a license for seven years during which it pays 40% royalties for an exclusive distribution license (which the author and producer split if the producer is retained for the fee-based production) and 25% royalties for a non-exclusive license.

This link takes you directly to the ACX "help" page for authors:

https://www.acx.com/help/authors/200484540

It used to be that Audible would only take books from publishers or book aggregators with at least five titles to create an account. ACX sidesteps this "rule" by acting as a book aggregator. In other words, you can submit your audio book through ACX as a single publication with no need for multiple titles.

This Worked For: As cited by ACX, renowned thriller writer M.J. Rose has used ACX for production and distribution of audio books for twelve of her novels. If it M.J. Rose, it can certainly work for you!

NOTE- While ACX does allow author/narrators to produce and submit their own audio books for distribution to Amazon, Audible and iTunes, it has very stringent requirements in place to ensure a professional product. See their "Rules for Audiobook Production" at:

http://www.acx.com/help/rules-for-audiobook-production/200485520.

So, you've decided you want to hire a production company to record your audio book. What, you ask, will it cost you? ACX does not allow you to price producers affiliated with their site before you "join" them, however, other research indicates that you'll pay between $1,500.00 and $7,000.00 depending on the length of the book, the cost of the narration, and the type of production. The cost at ACX will also depend on whether you are giving up partial rights to sales profit in exchange for reduced production costs.

Here are some other companies offering audio book recording/production services:

Reel Musician Pro- http://www.reelmusicianpro.com/audio-books.html A Nashville based sound studio. As per their Website: *as a Grammy nominated audio book production company, we do it all. From editing, abridging your audio book and script, to recording the voice over talent, adding custom or library music, award winning sound effects, audio trailers and video book trailers to delivering a fully designed and marketable audio book CD with artwork included if you desire - We Do it!*
For some approximates on the cost of studio and production time, Tom Gauger of ReelMuscianPro was kind enough to give us the following quotes for novels with the following word counts:

Middle Grade: 50,000 $1,500.00
Young Adult: 70,000 $2,100.00
Adult Novel: 80,000 $2,400.00
Sci-fi/fantasy: 100,000 $3,000.00

Please note, these quotes INCLUDE the cost of narration!

EdgeStudio-http://www.edgestudio.com/production/audiobook.

Audio Book Producers- Will tailor a package according to your needs. Services offered range from finishing of author narrated books all the way up to professional narration packages with distribution. Site offers fee splits for books were approved. The company states on their Website that they have distribution through Amazon's Audible, Amazon and iTunes.

Of worthy mention is Infinity Publishing's OneBook – Infinite TM:

http://store.infinitypublishing.com/product/onebook-infinite/. For a single price, $1,675.00, you get your book in three formats: print, eBook and audio. They will also distribute your book and provide some marketing support. Infinity's top of the line publishing product costs $5,199.00 which includes a lot of add-ones non in the OneBook – Infinite package.

Here's a link to the various packages: http://store.infinitypublishing.com/wp-content/uploads/2014/10/Packages_Compare.png As a cautionary note, in addition to paying these package rates, you also pay royalties of 30% for every eBook sale and 70% for every print and audio sale.

Fire-Up Your Book Sales With Gamification

"Gamification" simply means to add game design elements to make something more fun and engaging. Gamification is being used more and more by marketers and Web site developers as a tool to create interactive experiences that help drive consumer engagement and loyalty. It's also a technique being used to encourage desirable Web site usage behavior.

For example, if you want someone to watch your book trailer on your Web site, turn it into a game. Think of this strategy as an alternative to traditional advertising to get your message out. Right now, in today's market, where customers can choose to ignore advertising, we need alternatives. Game design elements - like offering points or rewards for reaching different levels of the game - can encourage consumers to do things that they normally consider tedious or boring like reading Web sites, learning, shopping, completing surveys or exercise.

Well, some of us find exercise tedious. Healthcare companies use this strategy; companies like Humana Inc. are providing incentives to members through game play to engage in healthy behaviors like getting preventive screenings, eating right and exercise.

Why are gamification strategies becoming so popular? In his recent book, "Game Based Marketing," co-author Gabe Zichermann maintains, "three generations of kids have now grown up playing video games as their primary source of entertainment - outstripping movies, music and books - and so the experience of playing games has changed their brains and style of interaction with the world." Keep this in mind when thinking about your target audience. Are they part of the generation that grew up playing video games? If the answer is yes, you should be paying close attention to this strategy.

Regardless of the age of your target, however, you can benefit by adding games and gaming elements to your marketing campaign. You will increase engagement with any age customer on your Web site, so they will want to visit, stay longer, tell their friends and come back repeatedly. Remember, it may take a few visits before they buy a book.

How can you apply gamification to sell your book? One way is to create an actual game based on your book. To do this well will require a significant investment in time and money. But, it's a great way to 1) continue the story so to speak, 2) potentially target new customers – reluctant readers may be attracted by a game, and 3) increase the shelf life of the book.

However, you don't need to create an actual game to take advantage of gamification. Another way to use this strategy is to apply gaming techniques - and parts of the game framework (such as levels, incentives, social networks, competition, etc.) - to your marketing campaign.

We cover several examples in the rest of this chapter that will give you some ideas for your own game plan.

Let's start with a recent example of how one publishing house used gamification to launch a brand new author with great success.

Vintage Publishing recently won, "Best Marketing Campaign of the Year," at the Book Marketing Society's inaugural Best Marketing Campaign of the Year Awards, winning for its hardback and eBook campaign for *The Night Circus* by Erin Morgenstern. The primary reason for the award? The book launch was accompanied by a game developed by Failbetter Games. "The on-line story world met the challenges of 21st-century publishing and book marketing head on: an innovative digital strategy that jointly built a new community for the book and extended the boundaries of storytelling itself on-line."

Fire Starter # 86-Gamify your marketing campaign

You don't have to spend thousands of dollars like the publishers of *The Night Circus* to apply this strategy successfully. Let's assume you wrote a book about antiquing: "The How to Hunt, Recognize and Buy Antiques" book. Instead of just reading about the hunt, you could include ten of the best antique stores in each region of the country in the book. The reader could have a passport and earn a stamp for each store he visits. Once he visited all ten in his region of the country, he could submit his passport for a prize. And guess who would stock the books in their stores? You may even be able to get the antique store owners in on the game to stamp passports. If you write a cookbook, you can gamify it by challenging readers to create a menu from your cookbook for a romantic dinner, picnic lunch or east coast inspired clam bake. Best menu wins a prize.

Let's bring this strategy down one more level; gamification can also be applied to something as simple as posts and status updates on social networking sites like Facebook and Google+. Here are some examples. Take major companies like Coke and JetBlue. Coke has been using gamification strategies in its status updates on Facebook, including URL riddles. Riddles are very popular as a way to engage people on Web sites.

JetBlue has been trying gamification strategies like "fill in the blank" updates. A post in March 2012 asked, "If your city could be any district, it would be _____. May the odds be ever in your favor." Classic!

And it's working. Evidently, JetBlue's fill in the blank updates "garnered 182% more comments per post than the brand's typical post," according to Simply Measured, a company that tracks social media platform data.

These strategies can work for you too. Over time, you may want to graduate from simple games on Facebook or your blog to creating more complex games based on your book content. But getting started with basic games should be easy: most Web developers are able to create simple gaming apps for social media, and this can be a relatively low-cost campaign.

Fire Starter # 87-Develop your game plan with these tips

1) Keep the games relatively simple; consumers get frustrated quickly if the game has too many rules or is complex and requires a lot of reading to get started.
2) Develop games that encourage consumers to come back. Adding levels to your game accomplishes this. Alternatively, incorporate a scoring system so the user is encouraged to improve his score over time.
3) Don't give away rewards for nothing; make your customers earn them. Research into human psychology tells us that people are happier when they earn something, rather than when we give it to them for little or no effort.
4) Encourage engagement on your Web site by giving bigger rewards for more engagement. For example, watching your book trailer earns them a discount on their first purchase. Watching the trailer and playing a game on your site earns them a bigger discount.

5) Develop a game with a viral element. Think of a pyramidal recruitment scheme that offers cool rewards and unlocks new parts of the story if the customer invites someone to play and if they in turn invite someone. This is obviously a higher-level technique but one that could offer great rewards if the game goes "viral" and spreads like wildfire across the universe at warp….well.

Well, you get the point.

The sky is the limit with gamification as a strategy for authors to market books. As a "creative," you are in a unique position to leverage the benefits of game techniques to sell books and gain customer loyalty. Using your creativity and skills as a storyteller (and world builder) you can come up with completely rare ideas - differentiating ideas that can help you stand out in a crowded market. So, get your game on! Start thinking about how you can add game design elements to your marketing strategy to attract and engage customers into brand new and exciting ways.

Let the games begin.

This Worked For: If you are not familiar with Scholastic's *The 39 Clues* series, then we suggest you study the publisher's multi-media marketing platform for this series as a great example of gamification and viral marketing strategies.

The series featured multiple books as well as related Web-based games, collector cards and cash prizes. The campaign was cleverly integrated to encourage the reader to buy more books; the books included hidden clues embedded in the book's pages. For example, *The Maze of Bones* included a series of mis-numbered pages that apparently spelled out a secret message. Furthermore, each book came with collectors' cards that could be used to find further clues in the online game. The online game involved solving a mystery to win a grand prize. The story also branches through products ranging from a board game to an iPhone app.

That is master class in gamification strategy!

Other Examples:

Puma: The World's Fastest Purchase

It's interesting to see how technology is seeping into everyday actions. In this instance, Puma has gamified shopping; the faster you make a purchase, the greater the discount. It's not exactly new, but in-store placement certainly puts a new spin on it. Bonus: the store can turn over a greater number of customers in a normal day!

Holly Lisle's Minecraft Spaceships

Author Holly Lisle created life-sized walk through models of spaceships featured in several of her books using the video game Minecraft. According to Holly, she made the models initially "to keep myself from making stupid location mistakes in the stories." Now, she is exploring the idea of offering the Minecraft models as thanks for buying the books" gift. This is a really creative idea, and we look forward to hearing more about Holly's customer loyalty and fan building marketing strategy.

Additional Resources:

For more study on gamification, check out *Game Based Marketing* (Wiley, 2012) co-authored by Gabe Zichermann.

Blaze A Path To New Markets With Translations And Foreign Distribution

$ to $$$- Minor to Major Bucks

Fire Starter # 88-Translate your book to find new markets

Translate your books to kindle interest in different countries and increase your distribution and reach, and ultimately, SALES.

In the last couple of years, Amazon has expanded into Spain, France, Italy and India. Other self- publishers, like Lulu, will distribute your book internationally. As a corollary, the Association of American Publishers reported recently that sales of eBooks in foreign countries increased by 333% between 2010 and 2011. With those kinds of numbers, every author should consider translating their books, so they can participate in this growing market.

In addition to sales figures, authors should evaluate UNESCO's United Nations Educational, Scientific and Cultural Organization-*Index Translationum* to gauge the overseas market for their work. You can find it at http://www.unesco.org/xtrans/bsstatexp.aspx.

The Index "contains cumulative bibliographical information on books translated and published in about one hundred of the UNESCO Member States since 1979. It totals more than 2,000,000 entries in all disciplines." You can search the database by a variety of methods, including the top ten countries translating into a target language, and the top ten authors translated in any country. The statistics provided from some searches can give you an idea about over-all marketing conditions. For example, a search of the top ten countries translating books into Spanish returns Spain, Mexico, Argentina, and the US in its top four. English is the top language translated into Spanish. In Spain, Agatha Christie and Isaac Asimov are in the top ten authors translated.

If you've been traditionally published but still retain your subsidiary rights, or if you are self-published, having your book translated into other languages may open up new markets. When seeking a translator, be sure to use one who is a native speaker of the target language and who has contact with the country of his native tongue. Because language evolves, only an active, native speaker will be on top of the current slang and usages. This will ensure that your translation reads as fresh, instead of stale and dated.

$$$ - Major Bucks

There are many professional associations which keep rosters of translators. One of these, the *American Translators' Association (ATA)*, https://www.atanet.org/ offers a free helpful buyer's guide

you can download at
https://www.atanet.org/publications/getting_it_right.php.

Another organization of worthy mention is The International
Federation of Translator. Find them here: *http://www.fit-ift.org/*

Another way to find a good translator is to go to the Amazon site in
the country you are targeting. Find translated works there and take
note when the author mentions the translator in their dedication or
when the translator has the status of co-author.

Typically, translators charge between 10 and 60 cents a word with
prices ranging between $4,000.00 and $15,000.00 depending on the
language and book length. About $36 - $50 a page seems to be the
average cost for books being translated from English to Spanish. To
reduce costs, you might try to request a referral from the English
department of a university in the country where your target language
is spoken. Once this translated version is obtained, you can then
offer the translated book for free from your Web site to native
speakers for feedback for a period of time, BEFORE you publish it
to a wider audience. This will enable you to correct embarrassing
translation mistakes before they are widely disseminated.

Here are some companies and individuals offering translation
services on the Web:

http://translator-login.babylon.com/FAQ2.aspx Babylon.com, the
language instruction/translation software company, offers human
translations for $140.00 per 1000 words. They do not price projects
exceeding that, however, do promise that the higher the word count,
the cheaper the project. At $140 per 1000 words, a 50,000 word
novel would cost $7,000.00.

http://www.b2btranslations.com/book_translation.html

http://www.proz.com/about/overview/jobs-directories/: Site has
directories, including translation companies, translators, students,
and more. The site states it has over 375,000 registered users.

http://www.translatorsbase.com/search.aspx?s=34&t=127: Directories of independent translators.

http://www.translatorscafe.com/: Directories of translators and translation services

www.thumbtack.com: Allows you to search for translators by entering in description of the project. Quotes from up to five translators are then emailed or texted directly to you.

$$ - Moderate Cost

 Another possibility is to offer a co-authorship or royalties for the translated version to a translator with a proven record. This will be easier if your book's English sales are healthy and consistent. Expect to pay a co-author half the net, while royalties on net to ghost translators may run you as high as 20%.

This Worked For: Author Scott Nicholson provided royalties instead of fees for the German translation of his thriller *The Skull Ring.* The book became a German best seller.

$- Low Cost

For the brave and cash-strapped, you can experiment with using translation software, but be sure to vet your translation from your Web site first by offering free copies to native speakers who speak English, and ask for feedback.

Babylon 10 advertises that it can be used to translate eBooks. This program is consistently an award winner by independent reviewers. See: http://translation-software-review.toptenreviews.com/ for a 2015 review of programs rating it as number one. At $179.00 for the program, it is definitely on the bargain end of translation solutions.

Another program is WhiteSmoke, which bills itself as the "World-Leading Leading English Writing Program," and includes translation software. See http://www.whitesmoke.com. It retails between $159.00 to $299.00 for the full suite, or you can purchase a license in increments of a month to a year.

Not quite ready to make the leap into translation? Feel like you need more information? Check out Amazon's translation resources with tips for finding translators and war stories from authors who've translated their works, here: https://kdp.amazon.com/self-publishing/help?topicId=A25ML2TL5OQQ11.

Fire Starter # 89-Distribute your book to foreign countries

$ - Low Cost

After paying to have your book translated, you'll want to make sure it's distributed to foreign countries with native speakers of your translated language. Here are a couple of ways to make sure that happens:

For printed books use Create Space's Expanded Distribution Channels.

At $25.00, this bargain is a no brainer. While all books published with Create Space can be distributed to Amazon.com, Amazon Europe and eStore channels, with Expanded Distribution your books will be distributed to bookstores and online retailers, such as Barnes and Noble, libraries and academic institutions through distributors like Baker and Taylor, and to certified resellers through Amazon's wholesale Web site. For details on eligibility requirements, royalties and how to sign up, see: https://www.CreateSpace.com/Products/Book/ExpandedDistribution.jsp

For eBooks, use a book distributor like Smashwords, Infinity, Kobo or Kindle Direct

Smashwords, Kobo and many other distributors of eBooks will distribute your books to foreign markets for fees ranging upwards of 10% or more. Infinity Publishing offers ala-carte distribution services for $249.00. They will distribute to Lightning Source, and Baker and Taylor Textstream to make your book available for purchase by libraries and bookstores worldwide.

While Kindle Direct does not charge an upfront fee for distributing to foreign markets, you do have to jump through several hoops to make sure your eBook is listed where it should be. Pay particularly close attention when uploading your book. There are two times during the upload process when you indicate your publishing/content rights. Together, these determine where Amazon will distribute your title. The first is in step one of the title set up process where you indicate your Publishing Rights. Make sure and check the box to indicate you own the necessary publishing rights. If you own world-wide rights, simply select that box, then make sure you select world-wide distribution so your book will appear in the kindle stores for the covered 24 countries.

Here's Amazon's explanation of that process:

https://kdp.amazon.com/self-publishing/help?topicId=A1H1OSSLAY4B4F and

https://kdp.amazon.com/self-publishing/help?topicId=A3BZH3BNSKZ0UX.

HOT TIP* You can also use distribution pages to limit distribution to foreign countries with native speakers of the language for the version of your book that is translated. One reason you would want to do this is to avoid having a book translated into French selling in Austria where it may do poorly.

HOT TIP* Be sure and establish an author's page for each of the kindle stores where your book will be sold.
HOT TIP* If you decided to use barcodes for your book, each translated version will require its own barcode.

Blaze a Trail to Your Web Site with Back links

Back links are an important part of your Web site promotion strategy and help you in two key ways: 1) they drive traffic to your Web site and 2) they help you rank higher in search engines. Simply put, back links are incoming links to your Web site or blog from other social media sites.

As you know, links to your site are an important way to build traffic, which in turn drives search engine rankings; the more links to your site, the better chance your site will be found via a major search engine. And of course, you want as many doors/portals to your home base as you can get so people can walk through and discover your amazing book. The "build it and they will come" strategy only works in a field of dreams. You need effective strategies to help you get links to your Web site or blog so people can find you and buy your book.

Before we get into strategies however, it's important to note that there is a lot of information on the Web about back-linking. We recommend you do your research and decide which strategies are right for you. In addition, we encourage you to stay away from strategies that smell like "link spam,"" and refrain from buying links. Yes, it is getting harder and harder to include links to your site in blog posts on other people's blogs, but there are some effective and "legitimate" strategies to help you build links and traffic.

Fire Starter # 90-Create content, content, content

The best way to get back links to your site is to develop high-quality content and share that content wherever you can. This is sometimes called "link baiting."

If you create high-quality content and post to blogs and your social media sites, you increase the likelihood that a popular high-traffic site will link to your site. You can also use Twitter effectively to drive traffic to your site. We covered this earlier in the book in the first section. All it takes is one link from a high quality, high-traffic site to generate significant traffic to your site and improve your search standings.

Fire Starter # 91-Partner with others to exchange links

Develop a Web link "network" with other authors or related businesses- authors in a related but non-competing genre- and all the partners' Web site traffic will grow. It's important to partner with writers or businesses who are targeting a similar demographic. For example, it won't help you to partner with an author or business targeting young adults if you are targeting 30+ women.

When it comes to businesses, look for complimentary products or services and think "outside the box." It's easier to come up with ideas for how-to books; if your book cover's antiques, approach antique vendors online. Another way to exchange links is to include other authors (or other partners) in your blog roll and ask them to reciprocate.

What's a blog roll?

A blog roll is a list of links to other blogs on your blog. Typically, this list of links is included on the sidebar of your blog. These links can represent related blogs or affiliated bloggers (check out wordservewatercooler.com) or can simply represent your personal favorites. Blog etiquette suggests that if a blogger puts a link to your blog in his/her or her blog roll, you should reciprocate.

Don't feel obliged; however, if you didn't initiate the link, and you don't approve of the content on the other blogger's site. Make sure to read the site, including archived posts and think about how the content of the other blog reflects on you and your brand before you initiate a link. A similar concept to exchanging blog roll links is exchanging banner ads. The banner ad acts as a portal to your Web site and can be designed with interactive features and audio to attract attention.

In general, when it comes to link exchanges, don't go overboard. Network and exchange links with sites that make sense but don't feel obliged to link to everyone who links to you.

Fire Starter # 92-Study your competitors

Study your competitors' blogs and Web sites to see who they are partnering with to get partnering/back-linking ideas for your book. Furthermore, there are back link tools (including **FREE** versions) that allow you to determine where your competitor's Web site traffic is coming from. Two popular ones are Open Site Explorer and Majestic SEO. Again, if the sites or communities linking to your competitors are a good fit for you, offer to provide an article or other content to enrich their sites or offer to be a "guest blogger."

Fire Starter # 93-Contribute consistently to other blogs

Post, comment and contribute to other people's blogs as much as possible. Becoming a regular, contributor-paid or unpaid-is a great way to build awareness for you, your unique talents and your book as well as drive traffic to your home base. While many blogs now use "no-follow" for embedded links, these links can still drive traffic to your Web site. In other words, links embedded in blog posts with "no-follow" may not help you in search engine rankings, they still help people find you and your book. Traffic can be driven to your site in multiple ways – a search is only one way. Additionally, if you are a regular contributor or guest blogger, the hosting site will typically allow you to link to your site in the byline.

Fire Starter # 94-Submit e-Zine articles

Article directories like e-Zine are a great way to build back links. Write a great article (you have the advantage here-there are a lot of non-writers submitting articles) and submit to these directories for inclusion. Since e-Zine manually reviews the articles, it's one of the most trusted article directories online. Once accepted, you will be given the opportunity to complete an author profile, including links to all your social media pages. Visit ezinearticles.com and check out the Authors' Spotlight in the sidebar. These writers earn front page status on the e-Zine site due to the number of high-quality articles they have submitted.

Fire Starter # 95-Interview or survey VIP's

Interviewing Very Important People (VIP)-including famous or influential people-will help you get links to your site and drive traffic. Surveys are an effective technique as well because you can ask multiple VIP's the same questions and contrast the responses.

The trick is to ask the right questions; timely and relevant questions that will result in unique content – content people can't get anywhere else. This type of content has a high chance of being shared with multiple links back to your site. In addition, the VIP will most likely link to the interview from their social media sites, and if they are influential on the Internet with a large platform, then a link back from their home base could really drive up your site traffic.

In general, people like to be interviewed, but it can be a challenge to get interviews with VIP's. You'll need to keep in mind a few tricks. 1) It's easier to get an interview when the VIP is promoting a new book or project. 2) Find a person close to the VIP and ask them their opinion; do they think the VIP would be open to an interview? What types of questions should I ask? When you do make contact with the VIP, you can name drop; "I talked to such and such, and they suggested you might be willing to do an interview." 3) Always act professionally when approaching a VIP for an interview. Some of us get pretty informal on social media sites, but it's best to remain formal and professional to show you're serious about the interview.

Use Publication Services Like "Free Days" To Get The Fire Started!

$ - Free For You and Your Readers!

Fire Starter # 96-Use "Free Days" advertising opportunities to jump-start your sales

When you agree to publish exclusively through Amazon Kindle Direct Publishing (KDP) Select Program, your book is added into KOLL, the Prime Member's lending library, and KU or Kindle Unlimited, which is a subscription service where for monthly fee readers can read all titles listed in the service, paying only the monthly charge. In exchange, you are given several publication services for free. These include the ability to purchase advertising (for more on this read above at *Light a Fire on Amazon*), Free Days and Count Down. With Free Days, you are allowed to sell your book for free for five days per 90-day enrollment period. With Count Down, you are allowed to offer your book at a discounted rate for a limited time. You earn a share of the KDP Select Global Fund based on how many pages KU or KOLL customers read of your book.

Go here to find the Amazon KDP Select FAQ:

https://kdp.amazon.com/self-publishing/help?topicId=A6KILDRNSCOBA

Combining your "free" days with other marketing efforts can result in a significant jump in sales. How does offering your book for free for a limited period of time help you sell more books for a profit? Free books draw a lot of traffic. No surprise there; people love free. You can use your free days to increase visibility, awareness, and word of mouth recommendations. Also, free days may help increase your reviews which will help with links, backlinks and ultimately search; search engines love links. Finally, people who download free books are avid readers and buy books as well. Free book days can help build your platform - one free book at a time.

This Worked For... US! In marketing this book, we've combined our KDP Select free days to coincide with attendance at writing conferences. We got the word out to attendees that in honor of the conference we were giving away the book for free. Our down-loads jumped considerably, one time enough to push us to the No. 1 position in our category! That position, coupled with the push to get the word out, resulted in considerable increased sales.

Don't just take our word for it! There is an entire cottage industry that has sprung up around Kindle free days. Check out these opportunities when planning how to optimize your free days:

$$ - Moderate Cost

Kindle Nation:

http://indie.kindlenationdaily.com/?page_id=642.

This site has various sponsorship options and the ability to target your sponsorship days to your free days. It also includes a spreadsheet with past sponsors' increased sales results on the site. Cost: between $29.00 for one day of a "book highlighter" that helps Kindle Nation readers locate your book on its free book days, and $229.00 for the Sponsorship Value Package which combines two other sponsorship products.

Digital Book Today:

$-$$$ - Free to Major Bucks

http://digitalbooktoday.com/.

The stated mission of Digital Book Today is to "Helping Book Lovers Find Authors in a Digital World." The company has been compiling "The Top 100 Best Free Kindle Books" updated daily since 2009. A minimum requirement for getting your book listed for free on the Top 100 list are 17+ reviews and at least a 4.0+ rating on Amazon. The site also offers paid promotional campaigns, with paid for ads starting at $15.00 and running upwards into the hundreds depending on length of run and ad placement. If you can't get your book listed on the "Top 100 Best Free Kindle Books List" during your "free" days, consider buying an ad on this page. The ads are relatively cheap and are obviously targeted at a prime audience.

Fire Starter # 97-Submit your book for the "Great Reads" FREE promotion opportunity

This is a weekly promotion offered by Digital Book Today; eight total authors are featured each week for one week. To be considered for the promotion you must have an Amazon rating of 4.0 stars or greater, a minimum of 15 reviews, and a price between $0.99 – $5.99. No novellas or short stories are accepted. The Web site claims "we offer this free promotional opportunity as a way of giving something back to the Indie author community."

Another **FREE** promotional opportunity is the "Guest Interview." This promotional opportunity requires an Amazon rating of 4.0+ stars, a minimum of 20 reviews, and a price between $0.00 – $9.99 on your book. Two interviews are posted per week on Digital Book Today. Currently, the site is scheduling 10-12 weeks ahead of the current date.

This Worked For: Tristan King, author of *Conquering Foreign Languages*, claims that the KDP Select Program increased his book sales by 600% in one week. Read more about his experience with this program and Free Days at Sean Ogle's blog here: http://www.seanogle.com/entrepreneurship/increase-amazon-kindle-book-sales

Stoke Your Fires Even Higher With Antic Advertising

The dictionary definition of "antic" is:
-a playful trick or prank: caper
-a grotesque, fantastic, or ludicrous gesture, act or posture
-fantastic, odd, grotesque

Does this sound familiar to you? Seen any advertising lately that fit the description above? We coined the term "Antic Advertising" to describe an advertising campaign that is designed purely to attract the public's attention and go viral. It can be in the form of an event, video, text message, article or blog, or it can be a series or combination of these things.

Antic Advertising campaigns are typically not designed to sell products meaning there is no strong call to action during the ad (no phone number to call to order); in some cases, the ads don't even mention a product or service. Many antic campaigns are actually one-off efforts and not part of a larger campaign or strategy.

Antic Advertising is about attracting attention--national media attention if you are really lucky--by doing or creating something incredibly *random, hilarious, controversial, clever, interesting, dangerous, surreal, crazy, sexy, scary, cool* (you get the idea). In other words, doing anything it takes to get the public's attention.

There are some key characteristics that we feel define a typical Antic Advertising campaign. Many are low-cost: the best of these campaigns rely on creativity rather than big budgets. The use of unconventional methods and tactics like mysterious installments or shock and awe videos or even flash mobs are also prevalent. And, as we said before, they are not usually part of a larger campaign or strategy.

"Viral marketing" is a related but somewhat different term. In our opinion, it's time "viral marketing" underwent some stratification. These days, not everything labeled "viral marketing" fits the bill. Viral marketing should be used to denote a marketing strategy that encourages people to pass along a marketing message or to share a product. The campaign is still designed to go viral but viral marketing involves a more thoughtful strategic approach with viral components seeded in the campaign. A classic example of a viral marketing strategy is Hotmail.

Hotmail was one of the first free Web based email services. At the bottom of every free email message sent out was the tag line, "Get your private, free email at Hotmail.com." So, every time a user of Hotmail sent an email, the marketing message was spread. Simple, but brilliant. And it wasn't about getting attention or national media coverage, it was about seeding the product with a viral component so it spread rapidly like a virus. That's a key difference between viral marketing and Antic Advertising.

Today, marketing antics have reached a new fever pitch. The stakes keep getting higher, the bar keeps getting raised. The pace and overall feel of these antic ads is more maniacal, fanatical and frenzied than strategic. And while many times these campaigns miss the mark--becoming so random or hilarious that no one is paying attention to the company or product--they can also be incredibly successful. And that's why we felt it was important to cover Antic Advertising in this book. It can be the cheapest form of advertising if it works and writers are uniquely positioned to take advantage of this strategy because success can be enhanced by an innovative and creative approach.

Please note it's not a strategy relegated to the small entrepreneurs with no budget or tech companies or movements or not-for- profits selling ideas. Not anymore. Today, staging antics to get attention and grab media attention is a widely used strategy by both large Fortune 500 companies and small up and comers. And the holy-grail is for the ad to go viral, meaning it spreads rapidly by "word of mouth" or "word of mouse." The former means the ad is spread verbally and the latter means the ad is spread electronically with a click of the mouse.

Whether you call it Antic Advertising or viral marketing doesn't really matter; what does matter is that you seriously consider this type of strategy. It can be incredibly powerful because if done right (and it works) your ads or marketing messages spread across the universe at warp speed. And the beauty is, the public is doing the spreading, not a high cost agency, so this type of advertising can be the most affordable form of advertising out there.

So let's review the goals of Antic Advertising

1. Create something that consumers want to share and therefore will go "viral"- you want people to talk about it and share it with their social networks. This means the customer is your sales channel and they are basically doing your marketing for you. It's no doubt an incredibly cheap way to get awareness for your name, book, or brand.

2. Create something that is newsworthy or interesting enough to get picked up by the national media. Free press by the national media is another really cheap form of advertising.

While Antic Advertising campaigns are typically spread online, they can be conducted on or offline. The examples below describe successful campaigns in both the on and offline environment and will hopefully give you some ideas for your own antic campaign:

Examples:

Blendtec "Will it Blend" Campaign

Blendtec was an obscure blender company until they launched the now famous campaign "Will it Blend." A series of videos - or infomercials- demonstrate the power of the blenders by grinding a variety of unusual items such as expensive electronics, glow sticks, golf balls and credit cards. The campaign has become an Internet sensation and continues today; check it out at willitblend.com. We especially like the icons that indicate whether it's safe to blend the item at home.

This is a really good example of the power of Antic Advertising because Blentec blenders were an unknown product (not unlike your book until you build awareness for it) and it was a relatively inexpensive campaign.

The Subservient Chicken

The Subservient Chicken was a promotion for Burger King's Chicken TenderCrisp sandwich and is often referenced as one of the first viral campaigns on the Internet that actively engaged millions of Internet users. Part of the "Have it Your Way" campaign, it began as a television ad with the tagline "Chicken the way you want it", but quickly migrated online. The Web site encouraged visitors to type commands like "sing" or "lay an egg" which an actor in a chicken suit would then follow.

The campaign was wildly successful (who doesn't like a man-sized chicken in garters acting out your commands?); although people questioned whether or not the Web site was actually hosted by Burger King. The genius of this antic campaign was in the interactivity with the audience which you obviously can't get with other advertising channels like print, radio or TV.

Sheep Art

Another big name company getting in on the antic advertising fun was Samsung. To promote Samsung LED, the company recruited a few Welsh shepherds, a herd of sheep, and a trained sheepdog or two. Throw in the LED lights- attached to the sheep of course- and you get a unique and clever video that went viral and received millions of views. Check it out on You Tube: http://www.You Tube.com/watch?v=bQr052_bSZA. And the video lives on: people are still talking about whether or not the images were "faked" which of course only adds fuel to the antic advertising fire.

Nike and Kobe

Nike hired NBA star Kobe Bryant to advertise their new Hyperdunk shoes with a viral campaign featuring videos of Kobe jumping over a bunch of crazy things, including an Aston Martin and a pool of snakes. Of course, the debate began immediately after the Aston video hit the Internet...did him or didn't he jump over a car heading straight for him, which is part of the reason the ad campaign spread virally.

Quicksilvers Dynamite Surfer

Several years ago, apparel company Quicksilver produced a video of some surfers attempting to create the waves they lusted for with dynamite. The video was picked up by the popular show Mythbusters (can you really produce waves with dynamite?) and the rest is explosive advertising history. What propelled this video in the first place? Well, who doesn't like to see something blown up or watch completely untrained people use weapons-grade explosives?

Smart Car: Ping Pong

Smart Car created a very clever way to demonstrate the responsiveness of their third generation electric car. They developed a gaming installation showcasing the cars as an integral part of a game of Pong. They promoted this "test-drive" event as the first game where cars are used as controllers. The event/installation was video-taped and uploaded to the Internet where it enjoyed viral fame. The video can be seen here on You Tube: http://www.You Tube.com/watch?v=lLCF54kXJrE

Having other people do your marketing for you is a very alluring idea; it's cheap and word can spread faster than any paid advertising campaign could hope to achieve. Therefore, for the author struggling to get awareness for their book in a crowded market, it's a potentially powerful opportunity, and one you should seriously consider. Remember, however, that getting attention with a headline grabbing publicity stunt is only part of the battle, albeit arguably the hardest part. After you have their attention, you need to know how to channel it into book sales. In marketing terms, you need to have a plan to engage the consumer after you have their attention. You should work to develop a consumer experience from end to end that continues after they buy your book. That's how you build loyal fans who will keep coming back to buy whatever you are selling.

This probably goes without saying, but all publicity (attention) isn't necessarily good publicity. You want to attract the right kind of attention and therefore, it's important that your Antic Advertising isn't offensive to the point that it negatively impacts your personal brand. Videos are probably the most popular medium for antic ads.

It's relatively easy and in- expensive to create a video with a digital video camera and upload to a You Tube account.

For the purpose of Antic Advertising, a homemade video less than three minutes long can be just as effective as a slick, over produced video created by a high paid agency. For proof, check out the Subservient Chicken ads mentioned above. You can edit your video with software like Windows Movie Maker to add titles or special effects. Really bad special effects can enhance your video if you're going for humor. And if you're technologically challenged, don't forget the kids. Many kids today know how to create a You Tube account and upload a video. Make it authentic, make it clever and unforgettable, and it won't matter a whit that it's not professionally produced.

We did a video for our Indiegogo campaign for less than 25 bucks and with basically zero know-how. Check out our process and end result at 100smallfires.com.

Now for the disclaimers. Will it work every time? No. Is it a gamble? Yes. There are no guarantees with this strategy; it can be hard to predict what will go viral. Some Antic Advertising campaigns are wildly successful taking a company or product from relative obscurity to a household word overnight. Others miss the mark entirely and sit in a dark corner of the Web never seeing the light of day. Is it worth a try? We believe so. But be prepared to experiment, and if you can afford it, try a few different concepts. Some will burn out but others may just start a blaze.

Remember that Antic Advertising doesn't always need to relate to the product; in your case a book. They can lean more toward the outrageous attention getting stunts. When thinking about creating an antic campaign, get creative. Here are some additional ideas to spark "out of the box" thinking.

1. Create a mock interview: write a script for an interview and have a friend or journalism major interview you on video and put the interview on You Tube. Make it funny, random, outrageous and poke fun at what your book isn't while at the same time, getting

across what it is.

2. Leverage famous campaigns that went viral like the "Will it Blend" Blendtec campaign. Blend your book.

3. Hold a contest for the best puppet skit of a scene from your book (aka the viral puppet videos with Harry Potter characters featured on You Tube), solicit input from the public and create a You Tube Channel just for these skits. Award a prize to the one that gets the most views.

4. Break a world record (if you are promoting a cookbook, bake the world's largest pizza).

5. Organize a protest related to a theme in your book. Or flip that idea on its head. At a book signing event, pay people to stand in front of the book store and protest you. Give them signs that say "Down with (your name). His book made us think and it hurt our brains." You will probably get noticed. You may even get coverage from the local media.

6. Create a flash mob event (doesn't have to be dancing or singing...what about a flash mob poetry reading?).

7. Spoof the life of a writer in a video; self-deprecating humor works well. Perhaps you make up a story about an author and their journey to creating and selling a book, but make it funny or create a satire. What stereotypes do people have about writers? We poke fun at writers- at ourselves- and our "masterpieces" in our crowd funding video mentioned earlier.

8. Build a series of videos around a theme and dole them out in installments to keep the public coming back for more. A good example of this is the Blendtec campaign mentioned above.

9. Don't forget the kids. If you need inspiration, find a teenager/young adult. They are tuned into what is currently going viral on the net and may be a well-spring of insights.

10. Check out Web sites like BuzzFeed and Viral Video Chart to see what's hot on the Web and what's going viral at any given time, to get ideas.

Here are a few **Fire Starter** ideas:

Fire Starter # 98-Humor is often successful in this type of advertising. What about a video/blog that cleverly demonstrates 50 ways to use your book; as a door stop, as a stool (stack them up), paperweight, fire starter, etc.

Fire Starter # 99-Consider inviting the public/your fans to create videos. In earlier chapters, we talked about the importance of engaging your customers or potential customers. This idea can apply to antic advertising as well. Develop a video contest; ask the public to create an Antic Advertising campaign for your book and give prizes to the top two entries. Make sure to display all entries on your Web site or author's page.

This Worked For: You may remember the Mentos/Coke geyser videos. If you haven't seen these, search for Mentos/Coke Challenge on You Tube. It's a great example of an Antic Advertising campaign using UGC (User Generated Content). Mentos created a contest and asked the public to submit videos of geysers created by combining Mentos with Coke.

Antic Advertising Worked For: Writers have been pulling antics to get attention for centuries. In the 2011 essay *How Writers Build the Brand*, author Tony Perrottet recounted several examples of how writers throughout history have conducted crazy stunts to promote their books including the following:

"Perhaps the most astonishing P.R. stunt — one that must inspire awe among authors today — was plotted in Paris in 1927 by Georges Simenon, the Belgian-born author of the Inspector Maigret novels. For 100,000 francs, the wildly prolific Simenon agreed to write an entire novel while suspended in a glass cage outside the Moulin Rouge nightclub for 72 hours. Members of the public would be invited to choose the novel's characters, subject matter and title,

while Simenon hammered out the pages on a typewriter. A newspaper advertisement promised the result would be "a record novel: record speed, record endurance and, dare we add, record talent!" It was a marketing coup. As Pierre Assouline notes in ["Simenon: A Biography,"](#) journalists in Paris "talked of nothing else."

Our fore-authors were no different from us and wanted the same things that we do; to create something that gets the greatest amount of attention in the shortest period of time with the lowest cost. We want our marketing messages to spread like wild fire at warp speed and create a large audience (attract a large amount of awareness) that is suddenly listening to what we have to say next. Again, the key is to know what you are going to do once you have everyone's attention. How will you to turn that awareness into consideration for you and your book? One option is to drive them to your email marketing campaign.

Final Note - on the spectrum of Antic Advertising, we recommend you stay away from crazy "stunt" marketing and focus on what you do best: creativity. You are a story teller so create a viral campaign that includes an element of storytelling and goes viral because it's clever, not crazy.

Sexify Your Book To Get Sales Smoking! Offer Alternative Versions Of Your Book, One Naughty, One Nice

You know all those intimate moments between your characters where you tastefully faded the scene to black?

Well...don't.

As demonstrated by E. L. James's *50 Shades of Grey* and progeny, sex sells... and sells and sells. According to Wikipedia, this best seller had sold over 125 million records worldwide as of June, 2015, and still doesn't show signs of stopping.

So, repeat after me with enunciation on the "Ss" please.

S-S-Sex sells.

Quit jumping up and down. Swallow your feeble protests. You know it. We know it. *Fifty Shades* proves it beyond a reasonable doubt. So if you want to increase your chances of success with a large demographic of the population, then consider this option. Really.

Now, we aren't telling you to re-write your novel to include gratuitous sex.

No.

Publish what you have - the balanced, tasteful version - but make sure you label this edition as PG or R. Then go through your book and add sex to each and every scene where its inclusion isn't utterly ludicrous. The naughtier, the better.

This is not the classic revision where you change things; this is letting your reader see places and actions that were cut off in your other version. If before you faded a scene with a kiss, go back and add more making out, and maybe some groping besides. If before you faded out a bedroom scene with your characters falling on the bed, go back and give the details of their hot and sweaty sex.

Call this your un-cut, X rated version and sell it in a brown paper bag cover with just a hint of the naughtiness inside peeking through a rip in the paper. Bring this version out a couple of months after you publish your first version, when the sales have started to slow down. Make as big of a fuss over it as you did over your first version.

Who will buy it? Well, just maybe you'll tap into that *Fifty Shades* crowd. After all, *Fifty Shades* started off as fan-fiction of Stephenie Meyer's bestselling young adult *Twilight* series.
Lesson to be learned?

If you don't sexify your work, your fans will do it for you, and maybe even make millions in the process.

Fire Starter (and we do mean fire starter) #100-Put sex on your cover

If you are not ready for the Full Monty, then consider putting sex on your cover. Publishers are replacing classic book covers with sexier versions to entice new and younger readers. As noted by Nils Kongshaug in his article, "Sexy Covers Lure 'Twilight' Teens to Capital-L Literature," three different publishers of books for teens have trotted out revamped classics – all featuring sexy modern covers. The new Penguin edition of Shakespeare's Romeo and Juliet features a modernized cover with a teen boy and girl in a pre-kiss embrace. Similarly, Penguin has put a brooding teenage Pip on the cover of Great Expectations. Sterling Publishing has issued a modernized, sexified version of Jan Austen's best sellers and Harper Teen has placed a huge blood red rose with the words, "Bella & Edward's Favorite Book," and says that this edition has outsold many new releases. See: http://abcnews.go.com/blogs/business/2012/06/sexy-covers-lure-twilight-teens-to-capital-l-literature/,

These publishers are breathing new life into classics by utilizing a smart marketing lure – sex.
So, the point here is everyone is doing it. The birds are doing it. The bees are doing it.

You can do it too.

If you have romantic elements in your novel, make sure those elements are reflected on your cover. Romance writers know this. Just look at a ten or so romance titles, and you will see quite clearly what they all have in common; men with abs - or rather their chests and chins - and just a touch of naughty. Titillating and eye catching and a real sales clincher.

Of course, you can also go with the symbolic object – a lipstick tipped cigarette, lipstick on a wine glass, a tie – a grey tie. Well, maybe not that one since it's been done to perfection already. But what about ripe fruit with a single bite taken out of it, ribbon strewn across another object, or a banana sitting between melons? (Can you tell how much we enjoyed writing this section?) OK, so they've all been done, and done, and done – but that's because they work. Isolate the sexual elements in your book and try to find a unique spin you can put on your cover.

Maybe you've written one of those books where it just isn't practical to intersperse your chapters with characters having sex. Well, there's still nothing to keep you from using the old bait and switch. You can still include a sexy, nearly naked model on the cover, maybe holding the first letter of your title; or a pair of pouty lips holding that letter between perfect teeth. There's a reason so many car commercial ads feature beautiful women - it sells. If the mere suggestion of sex can help sell a $60,000.00 dollar car, it should help sell a ten to twenty dollar book.

For That Matter, Do Alternative Covers

There's a reason large publishers do alternative covers, and even alternative titles, for books they market to other countries - culture and demographics affect the way readers view books. Research your demographics and experiment with different covers. This is most practical for eBooks of course. It's actually very easy to switch the cover of a Kindle book. So… just do it!

S-S-Sexify your book!

FINAL THOUGHTS

Everything is shifting in the world of publishing and book marketing. It's a transitional era and one that will not pass without some incredible misfires. With this kind of volatility, however, comes opportunity. So if you're feeling overwhelmed, frustrated, and perhaps even paralyzed by the sheer enormity of the marketing task ahead, don't give up!

Especially not now, because one thing we truly believe is the future belongs to you, the Creative. Consider the convergence of factors coming together at this very moment to create an environment ripe for the writer. Never before has there been so much access to books. Never before has the reader had the kind of power they wield today; the power to share their passion and become an advocate for writers and books, the power to shun the opinions of others, make up their own minds, and cast their vote for what they like and don't like.

Consider this; Corporate America is looking for good writers to tell their story-- to create content they can use to engage customers and develop long term relationships. Storytelling is one of THE hot marketing trends! As we have said earlier in this book, creatives are positioned very well in this new age of Content Marketing and Antic Advertising.

Now, consider this; many believe there is a backlash coming. A backlash against what we have become -- a Twitter nation of 140 characters or less. A backlash against the lack of depth in reporting-- there are scant few journalist these days helping us interpret the news, telling us why something is important, uncovering the truth. A backlash against the multi-tasking, mental stuttering behavior patterns we seem to have accepted as the "new normal." A backlash against "narrative deprivation"-- a term we heard used recently by Jessica Helfand during an NPR interview to describe how we are being deprived of stories in place of sound bites.

Finally, consider this; the antidote to what we have become is narrative depth. And who is better positioned to help us rebound from this backlash than you, the professional and passionate writer. You have been the quiet foot soldiers against the war on sound bites, carefully and patiently telling your story, unfolding your plot, describing the scene until we hear it and smell it and see it vividly in our imaginations. You are ready and willing to shed light on the truth, provide the depth we desire and tell stories that will stay with us a lifetime.

Get ready, writer.

Get a blog. Get a plan. Get your Press Kit!

Your future is here!

LIGHT A FIRE MARKETING PLANS FOR SMALL, MEDIUM AND LARGE BUDGETS!

Making an action plan with a budget is easier than you think. We've demonstrated how to use this book for planning with three example plans, one each for small, medium, and large budgets. Your personal marketing plan should focus on your strengths, but don't omit the areas where you think you are weak. So if public speaking is your forte, then make sure and include opportunities for that, but don't neglect social media sites like Twitter where your message has the potential to reach thousands.

LIGHT A FIRE MARKETING PLAN
FOR SMALL BUDGETS
(This is the plan used to market this book!)

LEGEND
PrP = PRE-PUBLICATION
PoP = POST-PUBLICATION
 # = NO. OF FIRE

EIGHT MONTHS OR MORE PRIOR TO BOOK BIRTHDAY PrP

Establish business entity (outside the scope of this book): consult a tax professional and/or attorney to determine what structure of business is best for you with regard to deducting expenses and declaring profits.

FOUR TO EIGHT MONTHS PrP:

$0 Researched target market, including blog sites for "how to" and craft books for writers.
$0 Created time-line and marketing plan for crucial events.
$63.93 Purchased domain name (1 year) and blog hosting (1 year) from GoDaddy.com.
$0 Set up blog site, and composed posts which we held until "launch" day.
$0 Signed up book name and companion name at www.twitter.com for twitter accounts.
$0 Set up one page Website our publishing company. Linked it back to blog site.
$0 Posted reviews for writer friends at Goodreads, Amazon and Shelfari.
$0 Updated personal Facebook account and set up Google+ site in personal name.
$$$150 Signed up for one writing conference for a time period immediately prior to launch.
$0 Started collecting/organizing emails into lists for launch day

notices and promos.

THREE TO FOUR MONTHS PrP:

$ Put together media kits and submitted to newspapers and magazines requiring a 6-12 week window.
$0 Put together an Indiegogo campaign together with a built-in budget for giveaways and promos. Held launch date on campaign until four weeks prior to book publication date.
$0 Put together a You Tube video introducing authors and project.

TWO TO THREE MONTHS PrP:

$0 Plotted blog book tour, gathering contact information and made initial contact.
$0 Reviewed Amazon's Top 1000 Reviewers and composed a list of at least 20 likely targets.
$0 Submitted draft of book to writing group for feedback and editing.
$50 Finalized book and formatted for Kindle using templates.
$0 Started working on a cover and alternative cover for "sexified" edition.

ONE MONTH TO BIRTHDAY!

$0 Ran Indiegogo campaign (crowd funding) for 28 days. Used cover art in promos and giveaways.
$$125 Purchased ISBN number from www.bowker.com for print book.
$0 Contacted list of targeted Amazon Top 1000 Reviewers who indicated could contact before launch day.
$35 Sent off for copyright online at www.copyright.gov.
$0 Wrote sales copy for listing on Amazon, and determined key words.
$0 Composed Author's page for later copying and insertion on book's birthday.
$$$250.00 Purchased promos for giveaways and blog tours.

YOUR BOOK'S BIRTHDAY!

$0 Published book on Amazon with KDP direct.
$0 Posted Author's page with previously written content.
$0 Posted to Social Media with previously written content.
$0 Filmed B-day video for later inclusion in You Tube or on Web site.
$0 Took lots of pictures for use in social media and posted some of them.
$0 Started blogging about marketing experience.

ONE MONTH TO TWO MONTH PoP:

$0 Award first Fire Starter of the Month Award.
$0 Contact post publication reviewers.
$0 Blog Tour!
$0 List book in Bowker's Books in Print.

TOTAL $673.93

LIGHT A FIRE MARKETING PLAN
FOR MEDIUM BUDGETS
(This budget is for a fiction novel with French characters)

LEGEND
PrP = PRE-PUBLICATION
PoP = POST-PUBLICATION
 # = NO. OF FIRE

EIGHT MONTHS OR MORE PRIOR TO BOOK BIRTHDAY PrP

Established business entity (outside the scope of this book): Consult a tax professional and/or attorney to determine what structure of business is best for you with regard to deducting expenses and declaring profits.

FOUR TO EIGHT MONTHS PrP:

$0 Submitted draft of book to beta readers for feedback and editing.
$0 Researched target market, including blog sites for MG books.
$0 Created time-line and marketing plan for crucial events.
$63.93 Purchased domain name (1 year) and blog hosting (1 year) from GoDaddy.com.
$0 Signed up book name and companion name at www.twitter.com for twitter accounts.
$0 Updated Web site to include blog and page just for this book.
$0 Caught-up on posting reviews for writer friends at Goodreads, Amazon and Shelfari.
$0 Updated personal Facebook account and set up Google+ site in personal name.
$$$150 Signed up for one writing conference for a time period prior to launch
$0 Started collecting emails into lists for launch day notices and promos.

THREE TO FOUR MONTHS PrP:

$0 Developed cover art, character art and logos for use in media kits, promos and giveaways

$300 Put together media kits and promo kits and submitted to newspapers and magazines requiring a 6-12 week window.

$0 Put together a Indiegogo proposal for book launch, together with a built-in budget for giveaways and promos.

TWO TO THREE MONTHS PrP:

$0 Plotted blog book tour, gathering contact information and made initial contact.

$0 Reviewed Amazon's Top 1000 Reviewers and composed a list of at least 20 likely targets. Reviewed Amazon's list of top French reviewers and composed list of 20 likely targets.

$50 Finalized book and formatted for Kindle using templates and mobi.

$$250 Purchased Bowker ISBNs

$0 Started working on an eBook cover and paper book cover.

$0 Ran Kickstarter for 45 days. Used cover art in promos and giveaways.

$ Contracted Create Space for print edition

$125.00 Pre-ordered 25 copies from Create Space so book will show up with a "buy now" button on birthday.

ONE MONTH TO BIRTHDAY!

$0 Contacted list of targeted Amazon Top 1000 Reviewers who indicated could contact before launch day.

$35 Sent off to for copyright online at www.copyright.gov.

$0 Wrote sales copy for listing on Amazon, and determined key words.

$0 Composed Author's page for later copying and insertion on book's birthday.

$$$350.00 Purchased/prepared promos for crowd funder related giveaways and blog tours

YOUR BOOK'S BIRTHDAY!

$0 Published eBook on Amazon with KDP direct.
$ Published print book with Create Space.
$0 Posted Author's page with previously written content.
$0 Posted to Social Media with previously written content.
$0 Filmed B-day video for later inclusion in You Tube or on Web site.
$0 Took lots of pictures for use in social media and posted some of them.

ONE MONTH TO THREE MONTHS PoP:

$0 Contact post publication reviewers.
$0 Blog Tour!
$0 Listed book in Bowker's Books in Print
$ Worked on getting French translator for French version
$$$1600.00 Contacted Audio producer for audio version
$0 After audio version available, used KDP free days plus stepped up marketing to increase sales
$200 Used Fire Starters with free days sales figures need a boost.
$150 Created first set of Birthday party and bling packs for sale from Web site.

$3,223.93 Total

LIGHT A FIRE MARKETING PLAN FOR BIG BUDGETS
(This budget is for any fiction book)

LEGEND
PrP = PRE-PUBLICATION
PoP = POST-PUBLICATION
 # = NO. OF FIRE

EIGHT MONTHS OR MORE PRIOR TO BOOK BIRTHDAY
PrP

Established business entity (outside the scope of this book): Consult a tax professional and/or attorney to determine what structure of business is best for you with regard to deducting expenses and declaring profits.

FOUR TO EIGHT MONTHS PrP:

$0 Submitted draft of book to beta readers for feedback and editing.
$0 Researched target market, including blog sites for MG books.
$0 Created time-line and marketing plan for crucial events
$63.93 Purchased domain name (1 year) and blog hosting (1 year) from GoDaddy.com.
$0 Signed up book name and companion name at www.twitter.com for twitter accounts.
$0 Updated Web site to include blog and page just for this book.
$0 Caught-up on posting reviews for writer friends at Goodreads, Amazon and Shelfari.
$0 Updated personal Facebook account and set up Google+ site in personal name.
$$$300 Signed up for two writing conferences for a time period prior to launch
$0 Started collecting emails into lists for launch day notices and promos.

THREE TO FOUR MONTHS PrP:

$0 Developed cover art, character art and logos for use in media kits, promos and giveaways

$300 Put together media kits and promo kits and submitted to newspapers and magazines requiring a 6-12 week window.

$0 Put together a crowd funder proposal for audio and translated versions of book, together with a built-in budget for giveaways and promos.

$0 Put together a video introducing author and project

$600.00 Researched blog tours and contacted and contracted for four blog tours

$700.00 devised plan for blog tour giveaways and purchased the same (Kindle fires)

TWO TO THREE MONTHS PrP:

$750.00 Researched paid for reviewers, and paid for reviews with Kirkus, publisher's weekly and several other credible independent review sites

$0 Reviewed Amazon's Top 1000 Reviewers and composed a list of at least 20 likely targets. Reviewed Amazon's list of top French reviewers and composed list of 20 likely targets.

$50 Finalized book and formatted for Kindle using templates and mobi.

$$250 Purchased Bowker ISBNs

$0 Started working on an eBook cover and paper book cover.

$0 Ran Crowd funder for 45 days. Used cover art in promos and giveaways.

$ Contracted Create Space for print edition

$125.00 Pre-ordered 25 copies from Create Space so book will show up with a "buy now" button on birthday.

ONE MONTH TO BIRTHDAY!

$0 Contacted list of targeted Amazon Top 1000 Reviewers who indicated could contact before launch day.

$35 Sent off to for copyright online at www.copyright.gov.

$0 Wrote sales copy for listing on Amazon, and determined key words.

$0 Composed Author's page for later copying and insertion on book's birthday.
$$$350.00 Purchased/prepared promos for related giveaways and blog tours

YOUR BOOK'S BIRTHDAY!

$0 Published eBook on Amazon with KDP direct.
$ Published print book with Create Space.
$0 Posted Author's page with previously written content.
$0 Posted to Social Media with previously written content.
$0 Filmed B-day video for later inclusion in You Tube or on Web site.
$0 Took lots of pictures for use in social media and posted some of them.

ONE MONTH TO THREE MONTHS PoP:

$0 Contact post publication reviewers.
$0 Blog Tour!
$0 Listed book in Bowker's Books in Print
$ Worked on getting French translator for French version
$$$3600.00 Contacted Audio producer for audio version
$0 After audio version available, used KDP free days plus stepped up marketing to increase sales
$200 Used Fire Starters with free days sales figures need a boost.
$250   Created Book club packs and listed at Web site
$1600.00 paid for English to French translation

$8,173.93 Total

SELECTED BIBLIOGRAPHY AND RESOURCES

BOOKS:

Avear, Michael. "Make a Killing on Kindle." Woodpeckermedia, 2012
GOOD FOR: Tips and tactics to maximize Amazon sales through key words selection and reviews. Advice on formatting for Kindle and how to extrapolate sales data.

Chandler, Stephanie. "BOOKED UP! How to Write, Publish and Promote a Book to Grow Your Business [Kindle Edition]." Authority Publishing, 2010.
GOOD FOR: Tips on marketing on the Internet; Detailed advice on managing social media, with a focus on Twitter, Facebook and LinkedIn. Bibliography included.

Coker, Mark. "Smashwords Book Marketing Guide." Mark Coker 2008-2011.

Fry, Patricia. "Promote Your Book," All Worth Press, 2011.

Howard, Johnson, Carolyn. "The Frugal Book Promoter, How to Do What Your Publisher Won't. USA, Star Publish 2004."
GOOD FOR: Detailed instruction on putting together a media kit, obtaining media interviews and traditional book reviews.

Kindle Direct Publishing, "Building Your Book for Kindle." Amazon
GOOD FOR: Detailed instruction on how to format your book for Kindle, including preparing the cover, uploading your book and previewing your book. Very limited information about metadata and entering key words. Additional reading on this topic definitely recommended.

Levinson, Jay Conrad, Frishman, Rick, Larsen, Michael, and Hancock, David. "Guerilla Marketing for Writers, 100 No-Cost, Low-Cost Weapons for Selling Your Work." New York, Morgan James Publishing, LLC, 2010.
GOOD FOR: An overview of how marketing principles can be applied to drive book sales.

Locke, John. "How I Sold 1 Million eBooks in 5 Months." Telemachus Press, LLC,
GOOD FOR: An inside look into how John Locke uses targeted marketing on his blog and Twitter to create an email list of dedicated readers of his series books.

Macarthy, Andrew. "500 Ways to Promote Your eBook Online: Internet eBook Marketing Tips to Sales Success for Kindle, Kobo, and More!" Andrew Macarthy, 2012.

GOOD FOR: Detailed insights on how to make the most out of social media, including Facebook, Twitter, Google Plus, Pinterest, LinkedIn and You Tube.

Matthews, Jason. "How to Make, Market and Sell EBooks All for Free." Jason Matthews, 2010

GOOD FOR: Detailed instructions on developing your blog site and Web site.

Nicholson, Scott. "The Indie Journey: Secrets to Writing Success." Haunted Computer Books, 2011.

GOOD FOR: Insights as to why a published author eschewed traditional publishing and how self-publishing eBooks enabled him to quit his day job to pursue his dream of writing full-time.

WEBSITES AND BLOGS:

Derek Canyon's blog, http://derekjcanyon.blogspot.com/. Good objective commentary on his trials and successes as an eBook author.

Create Space has tips on how to leverage the tools in Amazon to increase book sales. See: "How to Leverage Tools on Amazon.com to Increase Your Sales, Opportunities." Create Space Resources, 2010. https://www.CreateSpace.com/en/community/docs/DOC-1009 Author Marketing Ideas "helps the self-published and small print author maximize their marketing outreach to increase sales". They offer a no obligation and FREE review service called the Digital Footprint Evaluation to help develop a strategy for your online marketing efforts. Authormarketingideas.com

ABOUT THE AUTHORS

Sisters TK Read and Kathleen Vrona are successful entrepreneurs and have collaborated on a variety of projects including multiple Internet based projects. As early Internet pioneers, TK launched the first online mediation site and Kathleen co-founded one of the first Internet Service Providers in the Chicago Il area. In addition to launching new companies and services, TK writes middle grade and young adult science fiction novels. You can read more about her at www.tkread.com. Kathleen, in the meantime, continues a 25+ career as a marketing professional and is currently developing creative marketing strategies for a Fortune 100 company while writing in her spare time. For more on *100 Small Fires to Make Your Book Sales BLAZE!* visit them here: www.100smallfires.com .

DEDICATIONS AND SPECIAL THANKS!

This book would not have been possible without the support of many, many people. While we can't thank them all on these pages, we'd like to give a few special shout-outs.

Thanks to Connie Fleming for her fabulous clothes pin dolls we used to make our crowd funding video. *Arthur Author* would not have been half as cute if we'd gone with our original pencil concept. Connie, you're the best!

Thanks for the support of the WINGS, Southern-Breeze SCBWI group. Connie, Susan, Stephanie, Nancy, Maureen, we love you guys.

Thanks to our crowd funders, including Laura Wellman, Susan Spain, Barbara Brown, Camilla Zaepfel, Millisa Brown, Lawrence Ficek, and all those who chose to remain anonymous. Your generous contributions allowed us to execute our launch day promotion campaign.

Finally, thanks to all the authors and bloggers who inspired us and provided ideas and valuable reference materials for this book. We hope we referenced you and your work accurately in these pages.

www.ingramcontent.com/pod-product-compliance
Lightning Source LLC
Chambersburg PA
CBHW060030210326
41520CB00009B/1069